CRYPTOCURRENCY BITCOIN VS ALTCOIN, EXPLAINED TO MY UNCLE

OSCAR BUFF

Preface

A useful book for the layman and stimulating for those who navigate from one exchange to another, it has been written with the intention of not taking anything for granted, it is made so that it can be well understood, step by step.

The book is an introduction to cryptocurrency, and, simply, it tries to give more insights to bring the reader to have a good level of understanding of the subject, it explains how to make a wallet; how to buy, sell, and keep crypto coin savings; it talks about security, privacy, and how it is possible to earn money; compares Bitcoin with Altcoin; explains how exchanges and blockchain works; it discusses practical aspects; and, of course, couldn't miss the NFTs.

© Copyright 2022 All Rights Reserved.

Reference Number: 18490130922S068

Legal Note

All rights reserved. This book is under copyright and its usage is only for personal use, it is forbidden any reproduction with any technology.

Disclaimer

This publication does not want to entice anyone to do cryptocurrency trading or financial in general, this publication intends to provide an overview of what is a cryptocurrency, Bitcoin, and Altcoin and how this market moves, however, it is not exhaustive, is not complete, and cannot be used as a guide/book/map to do the financial activity, its contents are only for educational purposes.

To operate in the cryptocurrency and financial markets, you must be aware of the risks to which you expose yourself, and never do trading or financial activity of any kind with money you cannot afford to lose or are not willing to lose.

Cryptocurrency, Bitcoin, Altcoin, NFT, financial markets, currency trading opportunities, or financial products can have potential benefits, but likewise great potential risk.

Any references to possible outcomes that have happened or may happen are for the sole purpose of explaining an argument or developing a hypothesis but in no way claim that this is true, repeatable, or replicable.

All the approaches outlined here may not be appropriate for your situation—consulting a professional may be for you.

The author and publisher will not be liable for any loss of profit or other commercial damages including but not limited to special, incidental, consequential, pecuniary, or other damages

About the Author: Oscar Buff

Oscar Buff is a passionate and curious scholar who was born in London in 1969.

He grew up in a modest family in the Camberwell district.

Since childhood—when he went on holiday to France, having to exchange pounds for francs, and so doing the opposite on his return—he always noticed the differences in value on the exchange. With time, he began to study coins, and soon after he began to exchange coins online.

Among his studies, financial subjects have always attracted him; each study led to an experiment, e.g., trading stocks, investment funds, and ETFs.

Then, cryptocurrencies arrived, which he considers the money of the future.

He couldn't miss out on commodities with all their dynamics and interests behind every transaction.

Oscar currently lives in New Jersey. He likes to write books about his studies and experiences.

In his spare time, Oscar practices cross-country running, reads mystery novels, and sails when possible.

The author wishes to share with his readers the most effective strategies in the field of trading and offers his extensive experience that has been gained in financial investments.

TABLE OF CONTENTS

INTRODUCTION	**8**
CHAPTER 1	
WHAT ARE CRYPTOCURRENCIES?	**11**
UNDERSTANDING CRYPTOCURRENCIES	12
IMPACT OF CRYPTOCURRENCIES	14
HOW SHOULD YOU INVEST IN CRYPTO?	14
BROKERS FOR TRADING	16
HOW DO YOU CHOOSE CRYPTOCURRENCIES?	17
WHAT ARE SOME OF THE FUNDAMENTAL FACTORS?	
	18
CHAPTER 2	
COMMONLY USED TERMS AND THEIR MEANINGS	
	20
CHAPTER 3	
THE BLOCKCHAIN	**26**
BLOCKCHAIN AND THE EVOLUTION OF THE INTERNET	
	32
CHAPTER 4	
THE KING OF CRYPTOCURRENCIES: BITCOIN	**42**
HOW DO BITCOIN TRANSACTIONS GET RECORDED ON THE BLOCKCHAIN?	44
BITCOIN AS LEGAL TENDER	45
THE CHALLENGES FACING BITCOIN	47
WHY HACKERS ARE USING BITCOIN	48
CHAPTER 5	
THE QUEEN OF CRYPTOCURRENCIES: ETHEREUM	**50**
WHAT IS ETHEREUM?	52
MORE ON SMART CONTRACTS	54
DECENTRALIZED AUTONOMOUS ORGANIZATIONS (DAOS)	58
BITCOIN (BTC)	60

CHAPTER 6
MOST COMMONLY USED CRYPTOCURRENCIES   **60**

ETHEREUM (ETH)   62
LITECOIN (LTC)   63
RIPPLE (XRP)   63
DASH (DASH)   64
MONERO (XMR)   65
IOTA (MIOTA)   65
ZCASH (ZEC)   65
STELLAR (XLM)   66
NEM (XEM)   66
NEO (NEO)   67
TRON (TRX)   67

CHAPTER 7
THE RISING STARS: SOLANA, POLKADOT, AND BINANCE COIN   **68**

SOLANA (SOL)   70
POLKADOT (DOT)   73
BINANCE COIN (BNB)   76
ADVANTAGES   79

CHAPTER 8
ADVANTAGES AND DISADVANTAGES OF CRYPTOCURRENCIES   **79**

DISADVANTAGES   86
CRYPTOCURRENCY PARAMETERS TO ANALYZE IN INVESTING   87

CHAPTER 9
CRYPTOCURRENCY MINING   **100**

CHAPTER 10
BITCOIN WALLETS, STORAGE, AND TRANSACTIONS **111**

THE PUBLIC KEY   113
THE PRIVATE KEY   113
CREATING A BITCOIN WALLET   115

ONLINE WALLETS	116
CHOOSING THE BEST WALLET	118
HOW DO I GET BITCOIN?	118
WHERE DO BITCOINS COME FROM?	119
BUYING BITCOIN	120
CENTRALIZED AND DECENTRALIZED EXCHANGES	125

CHAPTER 11
CRYPTOCURRENCY TOP EXCHANGES — 125

CRYPTOCURRENCY EXCHANGES TO CONSIDER	127
OTHER TOP EXCHANGES TO CONSIDER	139
CHOOSE A CRYPTOCURRENCY BROKER OR CRYPTOCURRENCY EXCHANGE	144

CHAPTER 12
HOW TO BUY A CRYPTOCURRENCY — 144

BUYING CRYPTOCURRENCY IN OTHER WAYS	150

CHAPTER 13
CRYPTOCURRENCY TRADING — 159

HOW TO READ THE GRAPHS	163
THE TECHNICAL ANALYSIS	166
SUPPORTS AND RESISTANCES	169
RELATIVE STRENGTH INDEX (RSI)	173
MOBILE MEDIA	177
MACD	181
THE ANALYSIS BASIC IN MARKET OF THE CRYPTOCURRENCIES	184

CHAPTER 14
INITIAL COIN OFFERINGS (ICOS) — 190

INITIAL COIN OFFERING DEFINED	191
HOW ICO WORKS	194
INITIAL COIN OFFERING VS INITIAL PUBLIC OFFERING	196
PROS AND CONS OF ICOS	198
HOW TO SPOT AN ICO SCAM	200

SCOUTING FOR THE BEST ICO LAUNCHING SERVICE
     COMPANY   200
WHAT'S DEFI?   202

CHAPTER 15
DEFI, DAPPS, AND NON-FUNGIBLE TOKENS   **202**
WHAT ARE DAPPS?   206
WHAT ARE NON-FUNGIBLE TOKENS?   207

CHAPTER 16
ADOPTION AND THE FUTURE   **217**
CURRENT TRENDS IN CRYPTOCURRENCIES   218
UPGRADES IN SCALABILITY AND ANONYMITY   220
BITCOIN AND GAMING   222
BLOCKCHAIN'S IMPACT ON INDUSTRIES   223
THE ROLE OF WOMEN IN BITCOIN AND BLOCKCHAIN
     TECHNOLOGY   227
HOW CRYPTOCURRENCY AND BLOCKCHAIN ARE
     CHANGING THE FINANCIAL INDUSTRY   228
CRYPTOS IN THE NEXT DECADE   230

CONCLUSION   **232**
                                                       232

INTRODUCTION

Cryptocurrency is otherwise known as a crypto asset. This is a medium of exchange that is used to control the creation of new units through secure transactions. Cryptocurrency is an alternate currency that is actually a digital currency such as Bitcoin. Ultimately, Bitcoin was the first decentralized cryptocurrency back in 2009. Since then, several cryptocurrencies have been created such as altcoins. Altcoins are a blend of alternatives to bitcoins.

As stated, cryptocurrencies are decentralized which means that it is much like the blockchain used by Bitcoin's transaction database as far as using a distributed ledger goes. This also means that it does not run like normal banking systems that are centralized.

An anonymous electronic cash system was first published back in 1998 by Wei Dai which was called "b-money." Not too long after that, Nick Szabo created what was known as "Bit Gold." Much like Bitcoin, Bit Gold requires its users to complete work functions with solutions that are put together and published. A currency system that was based on the reusable proof of work was created by Hal Finney who used Wai and Szabo's work as inspiration.

Bitcoin which was created by Nakamoto used a cryptographic function (SHA-256) that allowed it to work as a proof of work system. Alternatively, in 2011 another system called Namecoin was created as an attempt to help DNS decentralize. Doing this would make Internet censorship extremely hard. Not too long after Namecoin was released, Litecoin was also released. This became the first cryptocurrency to use scrypt as its hash function. Even again, a hybrid that used proof of work and proof of stake was created called Peercoin.

Although several different cryptocurrency programs have been created, very few have actually ended up being successful. Back in August of 2014, the treasury department in the UK announced that they had been studying cryptocurrencies and what role they could end up playing in the UK economy.

Also in 2014, the second generation of cryptocurrency programs—such as Monero, Ethereum, as well as and NXT—was presented to the public. These programs have some advanced functions that they use such as side chains, smart contracts, and stealth addresses.

Just like blockchain, cryptocurrencies are threatening the price of credit for financial institutes. Along with this, the more trade that happens with cryptocurrencies is going to cause the consumer to lose their confidence in fiat currencies. Because of the widespread use of cryptocurrencies, it is going to make it more difficult for financial institutions to gather the data that they need—as far as the economic activity is—which is what helps the government to steer the economy.

It has been stated by a senior banking officer that the "widespread use of cryptocurrency makes it more difficult for statistical agencies to gather the economic data that they require."

On February 20, 2014, the very first Bitcoin ATM was launched by Jordan Kelley (who is the founder of Robocoin). This ATM is located in Austin (Texas) and is just like a bank ATM, but the scanners instead read some form of government idea in order to confirm their identification. This ATM was used just like any other bank ATM, except that it would allow the user to gain access to any cryptocurrency that they had in their account.

CHAPTER 1

WHAT ARE CRYPTO-CURRENCIES?

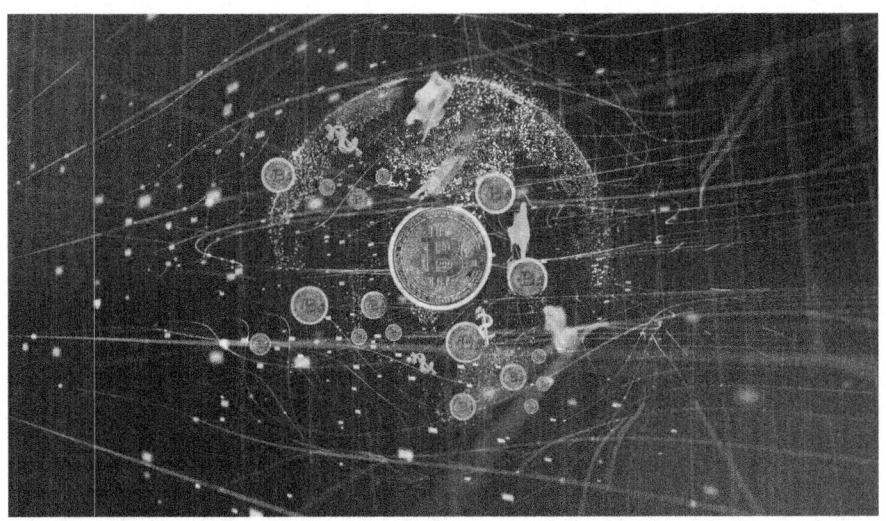

Image by Tamim Tarin

C ryptocurrencies are decentralized digital assets that can either be used as a medium of exchange or as a store of value. Cryptocurrencies run on blockchain technology that uses a distributed public ledger to verify all the ownership records using a consensus mechanism.

Unlike the regular fiat currency, cryptocurrencies don't exist in paper form and are not controlled by any central institution. For example, USD is managed by the Federal Reserve Bank, and the decisions made by the Feds can either appreciate or depreciate the value of the USD as a currency. On the other hand, cryptocurrencies, such as Bitcoin, cannot be influenced or manipulated by any financial institution or government.

Understanding Cryptocurrencies

To invest smartly in cryptocurrencies, you need to know about blockchain technology and different consensus mechanisms. The blockchain technology that powers cryptocurrencies use a complex mechanism to create a distributed ledger that cannot be tampered with or hacked.

Real-Life Example

Sam is intrigued by cryptocurrencies and decides to try them for a real-world transaction. He installed a cryptocurrency exchange called Binance to help him buy cryptocurrencies in exchange for fiat currencies. He researched and found out that a nearby bookstore accepts cryptocurrencies as a payment method and purchased five books worth 100 USD.

He opened his crypto-exchange app and scanned the QR code to pay a total of 0.0031 Bitcoin, equivalent to 100 USD. The transaction happens in seconds, but many processes involve verifying and embedding the transaction into the blockchain. When Sam scans the QR code, the cryptocurrency exchange triggers an event to confirm whether Sam's account has sufficient funds to make the transaction. Sam will have both a public and private key to secure his account.

Once the verification of funds is done, the transaction will happen. Users (known as miners) present in the network will verify the transaction by solving a mathematical problem involving energy consumption. Once a miner verifies the transaction, they will inform everyone on the network, and when everyone agrees that it is a valid transaction, it goes into a block. It will then forever exist in the blockchain public ledger.

This process usually takes 30 minutes. Once a block is placed in the blockchain, it cannot be tampered with or modified. All the transactions will become immutable, and hence, prevent a double-spending problem when the same digital token gets spent more than once. Miners will receive a reward for verifying the transactions.

However, remember that cryptocurrencies are not anonymous but rather are pseudonymous. Everyone in the blockchain network can view your transaction records to link them to your identity.

Impact of Cryptocurrencies

In 2009, when an unknown entity named Satoshi Nakamoto first introduced Bitcoin in their white paper, everyone was confused about how it could work in the real world. The dark web first popularized Bitcoin as an exchange value, and within the next few years, the popularity of Bitcoin increased exponentially. Since then, the world has seen a rapid advancement in cryptocurrencies and blockchain technology.

Cryptocurrencies are considered the most profitable financial instruments for investors and are a speculative bubble by some Wall Street big heads. While it is true that there is volatility in the movement of cryptocurrency prices, it isn't a bubble.

How Should You Invest in Crypto?

Like every other financial instrument, you must use either an exchange or broker to buy and sell your cryptocurrencies. It is easy to exchange Bitcoins using a wallet software, however, it becomes a problem when you want to use your fiat currency to buy cryptocurrencies. You need to go through a mediator, such as an exchange, which provides a medium to exchange cryptocurrencies.

All the software and digital access necessary for starting a cryptocurrency exchange are available in the open-source domain as a decentralized currency. Hence, there are a lot of developers trying to provide Bitcoin exchange platforms. With many options available, you need to be very strict about looking out for the factors described below whenever using one of these exchange platforms.

Security

Cryptocurrency exchanges need a high level of security, as many scammers are trying to lure investors into phishing their accounts and drawing their funds. Due to this reason, you need to choose a cryptocurrency exchange that saves all the funds deposited in cold storage so that no hacker can access them.

Supported Cryptocurrencies

Usually, cryptocurrency exchanges only support some of the popular cryptocurrencies. Due to liquidity problems, money exchanges don't provide you with the right to invest in low-cap cryptocurrencies. Before creating an account with a cryptocurrency exchange, make sure that they support all Forex and crypto pairs so that you can have liquidity for the currency of your choice.

Fees and Customer Service

Cryptocurrency exchanges usually charge transaction fees based on liquidity and demand for cryptocurrency transactions. Usually, they charge fewer fees for crypto pairs and more charges for Forex or crypto pairs. Good customer service is also an important prerequisite for a crypto investor.

You can also open your account with decentralized cryptocurrency exchanges that offer more safety as the platforms themselves run on the blockchain platform. However, decentralized cryptocurrency exchanges are still in a novice stage, and there is very little liquidity, especially for altcoins such as Cardano.

Binance and Coinbase are some of the popular cryptocurrency exchanges right now in the market.

Brokers for Trading

While exchanges are used to invest in cryptocurrencies from fiat currencies, brokers can help you speculate on the cryptocurrency market. Brokers also provide a high liquidity rate for traders with a small transaction fee. Using brokers, cryptocurrency investors can either make long or short positions according to their requirements.

The only difference between brokers and exchanges is that you will not own any asset in your trading account. Brokers will provide you with high leverage operations. Ensure that your broker is regulated, as many scams are happening due to little restriction from the government.

Both brokers and exchanges will provide web wallets to your accounts. These wallets can help you to store both public and private keys. Installation of wallet software or deterministic wallets can be a great way to secure your Bitcoin accounts.

How Do You Choose Cryptocurrencies?

Bitcoin and Ethereum mostly occupy the market capitalization of cryptocurrencies. To find other alternative cryptocurrencies to earn quick returns, you need to follow a strict pattern that has been deemed successful for a lot of crypto investors:

Research

First, you need to do a lot of research about cryptocurrency. Start with its white paper and understand what problem it is solving. If there is no motive to solve a problem, there are fewer chances of that cryptocurrency's success.

Research should involve a detailed fundamental analysis of details such as market capitalization, volume, and historical prices. Many investors and speculators also depend on traditional technical indicators, such as the MACD (Moving Average Convergence Divergence) indicator, to estimate the future movement of the cryptocurrency.

Accumulation and Distribution

Once you have chosen at least 5 alternative cryptocurrencies using different research techniques, you then need to prioritize these cryptocurrencies based on your fundamental analysis research. As alternative coins are very volatile, you need to distribute them based on their strengths and weaknesses. Using advanced technical skills, such as Fibonacci extensions and support resistance levels, can help investors during this stage.

Investors can also use sentimental and capital analysis techniques in correlation with fundamental and technical analysis to increase their successful predictions.

What Are Some of the Fundamental Factors?

All the fundamental factors mentioned below can be easily obtained using online services. If you want to analyze these factors for many alternative coins, then we suggest you use:

Number of Transactions

Carefully analyze the number of transactions that are happening every day in the blockchain. If there is a decrease in the number of transactions, you should find out why.

Active Addresses

The popularity of cryptocurrency is also determined by the number of active addresses in the blockchain ecosystem. If there is an increase in the number of active addresses, we can understand that active users use it as a transaction medium.

Volatility

Volatility is also an important fundamental factor when considering whether to invest in a cryptocurrency. If cryptocurrency's price always changes, then it is not a good investment choice.

Liquidity

As a cryptocurrency investor, you need to be aware of the liquidity potential of a cryptocurrency. If not, you will not be able to sell your coins during a crash and can partially hold cryptocurrencies with negligible value.

Besides these fundamental factors, consider market capitalization, mining, and "hash power" (computational power) before choosing a cryptocurrency for investment. Hash power, or the hash rate, is the term used to describe the combined computational power of a specific crypto network or an individual mining rig on that network.

CHAPTER 2

Commonly Used Terms and Their Meanings

- **Bitcoin:** A cryptocurrency that was invented in 2009 by pseudonymous Satoshi Nakamoto.

- **Cryptocurrency:** A digital asset designed to work as a medium of exchange. It usually has a value that can be equated to physical currency.

- **Blockchain:** A public ledger that records bitcoin or any other digital transactions.

- **Mining:** Refers to the process of gaining more bitcoins by using computer processing software to uncover new bitcoins with no money necessary to start.

- **Stocks:** Represents ownership of a fraction of a corporation.

- **Wallet:** A storage device, digital or physical that holds cryptocurrency and can sometimes offer encrypting and signing capabilities.

- **Algorithm:** A set of calculations that are used by a computer to solve problems.

- **Fractional-reverse banking:** This represents only a portion of deposits at a bank backed by physical currency available for withdrawal.

- **Block number 0:** The first Bitcoin block.

- **BTC:** Abbreviation for "Bitcoin"

- **Central bank:** A bank that provides money services regulated by the government.

- **Peer-to-peer:** Refers to a bitcoin network that is reliant on user-to-user exchanges without the use of go-betweens.

- **Coinbase:** A platform for buying, selling, transferring, and storing digital currency.

- **Bitpay:** This is a payment processor used specifically for the cryptocurrency known as Bitcoin.

- **Fork:** This refers to when a blockchain splits due to a block that is found by multiple miners at the same time, usually involves a shift in the protocol, resolved by the longer chain absorbing the shorter chain.

- **Miner:** A person actively trying to uncover new bitcoin units through computer programming and software.

- **Payment processor:** Software designed to accept payments and transactions using digital currencies.

- **Fincen:** Financial crimes enforcement network, part of the United States Department of the treasury, which purpose is to prevent financial crimes.

- **Money services business:** Any business involving money such as currency exchanger, check casher, money transmitter, or issuer/seller of traveler's checks and money orders.

- **Bitcoin faucet:** A website or software that rewards users in the form of satoshis for completing a task.

- **Captcha:** A spam protection system used to differentiate computers from humans when entering data.

- **Bitcoin network:** A network specifically used for the

exchange of bitcoins from user to user.

- **Ledger:** A book where account transactions are recorded.

- **Bitcoin address:** The digital address that a bitcoin gets registered to, which is created by picking a random private key.

- **Altcoin:** A term used to describe all other cryptocurrency units launched after the creation of bitcoin.

- **Transaction:** Designated input and output of bitcoins between users.

- **Private key:** Used in the exchange of bitcoins and paired with a public key. The bitcoins under this key become unusable if the private key is lost.

- **Public key:** Used to publicly sign for the exchange of bitcoins, generated using the bitcoin algorithm and paired with a private key.

- **Satoshi:** A fraction of a bitcoin worth one-hundredth of a millionth of a bitcoin, named after the pseudonymous creator of bitcoin.

- **Fiat money:** Government-issued currency, such as the US dollar. Does not need to be backed by a commodity.

- **Crypto-yield:** Also known as yield farming, is the practice of lending crypto assets to create a high return in the form of more cryptocurrency.

- **Digital currency:** A currency that exists solely online but can carry an equivalent value to a fiat currency. Can be spent like fiat money through the use of special payment processors, the value increases or decreases based on transactions as well as the value of the digital currency unit at the time.

- **Electronic money:** It's the electronic equivalent of fiat money whose value increases or decreases based on transactions.

- **Hash:** A 64-digit hexadecimal number that is used to solve part of the bitcoin mining process equation.

- **Hexadecimal:** A numeral system using a base of 16 rather than the common decimal system that uses a base of 10.

- **Cryptography:** Also known as cryptology, it is the practice of storing and exchanging information in a private and secure way.

- **Encryption:** The process of taking an intelligible message and turning it into an unintelligible form.

- **Cipher:** A tool used to decode an encrypted message or algorithm.

- **Decryption:** The process of returning an encrypted message back to its original form.

- **Cryptanalysis:** The process of studying encrypted codes in hopes decrypt them.

- **Broker:** A person who buys or sells goods for others.

- **Diversification:** To have a range of stocks and investments in order to minimize risk.

- **Common stocks:** A form of ownership in a company, also known as company shares.

- **Bonds:** A government or company-issued contract when borrowing large sums of money.

- **Preferred stocks:** A form of ownership in a company also known as company shares, preferred stockholders are entitled to a fixed dividend as payment.

CHAPTER 3

THE BLOCKCHAIN

Blockchain technology is most often associated with Bitcoin, but the distributed ledger has uses far beyond cryptocurrency. A blockchain is a distributed database of records stored in "blocks," which are linked together to form chains. The blocks are secured using cryptography and grouped into irrevocable chains with each block signed by both the creator and several nodes from the network.

Essentially, blockchain technology allows every computer on the network to share one distributed ledger among themselves. This eliminates intermediaries that traditionally provide trust between people or organizations trading goods or services.

Blockchain technology could have a similarly profound impact on industries from banking and finance to logistics and energy. The way we own property in the future could look a lot different—if blockchain enters the mainstream in a big way, it may not be long before we could see all sorts of new business models.

Why would someone want to use it? Blockchain is essentially a shared record-keeping system that combines elements of cryptography, peer-to-peer networks, and the open-source movement. It is basically a distributed ledger that can serve as the basis for creating value by recording transactions between parties without the need for third parties to conduct those transactions between them. For example, a blockchain could be used to store medical records or proof of identity for a financial account.

Blockchain solutions can provide new ways to store business data and machine-to-machine interactions between machines. This allows the sharing of information without requiring a central authority for validation of that information, opening blockchain solutions to many new types of organizations—from small enterprises to multinational companies.

In the transportation industry, smart contracts could replace the entire driver's license and vehicle registration process by creating a driverless car on a blockchain network. With this shared ledger, the car would only respond if it is moving forward within certain parameters of speed and location. The car decides where it is going and who is operating the vehicle based on that shared record.

Storing records on a blockchain also means that data can be distributed more broadly across different organizations. A distributed ledger of records provides an immutably secure way for different organizations to share information without having to reconcile it with any central authority. What's more, blockchain solutions could make it easier to verify the authenticity of data whether that data is medical or financial records or election results.

The implications of blockchain technology go far beyond cryptocurrency, however, with hundreds of new businesses launching every year to disrupt traditional industries. This includes startups using blockchain technology to create entirely new ways to move money, invest, buy property, secure contracts, trade goods, and much more.

A potential problem with decentralized systems is performance. Blockchains are always slower than centralized databases. This means that processing occurs at the speed of the network itself rather than at the speed of a centralized computer. Blockchain networks can process large amounts of transactions but it takes time for their distributed ledgers to update across the network. Although this may not be a problem for some applications or users, it may be impractical or too slow for others. For example, transactions may take too long for large amounts of money, or the process may need to be repeated over and over again when processing multiple transactions.

For that reason, blockchain networks are often combined with another distributed database technology known as a replicated database. A replicated database is essentially an alternative version of the ledger stored in each node of the network. This allows the blockchain to continue to process new transactions without waiting for an entire network consensus to occur. Replicated databases may also provide faster transaction processing speeds than blockchain ledgers.

While many companies are experimenting with blockchain technology, not everyone is convinced it's here to stay. Simon Taylor, chief executive officer of the UK-based blockchain startup Tango, said that it's "immature technology" that's "more hype than reality." However, he doesn't see this as a reason to be dismissive of it.

Taylor says that blockchain will very likely revolutionize how we do business in the coming years because it will make two things possible. The first is bringing currency into the digital age by giving currency the same degree of traceability and incorruptibility as any other kind of data. The second is creating new forms of business models by allowing all transactions to be recorded in one database which can then be shared with others or traded within an ecosystem.

The company is working on a product that makes it easy to create these new business models by allowing anyone to create their own applications on Tango's network. These applications can then be driven by the companies' own transactional records, which are stored on the blockchain. So they can be easily shared with others or traded within an ecosystem.

Taylor says that this allows companies to build ecosystems of startups based upon their own infrastructure of data. For example, Tango's current app tracks its drivers' movements with their low-cost wearable devices and provides instant feedback for better routes driven or cheaper services provided. It's a data-sharing app that can be used by any number of companies in the future.

The technology is being deployed at a large scale in several industries today, including financial services, healthcare, telecommunications, media and entertainment, automotive, government, and others. Some of these applications are already becoming reality with the application of blockchain to finance.

Cryptocurrency is one industry with significant use cases. But it's not the only one. A blockchain-based voting platform is being used in Estonia with 250,000 citizens using it for elections under an e-residency program. In the US, a blockchain-based platform was used to secure the distribution of thousands of tickets for a recent music festival. The Singapore national stock exchange is using a blockchain to track the transfer of assets and derivatives trades. IBM and Maersk are using a blockchain solution to create an international shipping tracking service. And Walmart has announced that it added several Chinese companies to its China food tracking solution that uses blockchain technology to trace the movement of food from farm to store shelves.

Blockchain technology also offers tremendous potential in supply chain solutions for oil and gas, mining, and commodities trading companies such as Cargill and Louis Dreyfus Commodities. The technology can also be used to record shipping transactions or verify the authenticity of luxury goods. Blockchain-based solutions are already being deployed to secure identity documents and track ownership of luxury goods.

The Internet has brought much convenience and speed to our daily lives. But it has also created many challenges for businesses who must now deal with a much more complex web of dependencies, far-flung partners and third-party vendors, broken processes, low supplier transparency, untrusted middlemen, and mistrust between parties. That's why blockchain may have widespread adoption in the coming years as one way to put businesses back in control of their operations by connecting everyone on the network.

Blockchain technology allows individual users to function as their own banks, in charge of processing transactions, storing funds, and providing financial services without the need for a third-party intermediary.

It is quite an ingenious idea that has both excited us and given us pause at times. Despite this potential for good, there are areas in which it could disrupt the way things currently operate. One of the first areas of concern is privacy. It is one thing to have our privacy put at risk by data breaches on large social media sites, but to do so in relation to an entire economy is quite another matter altogether.

This will go through some of the potential impacts that blockchain technology may have on our financial lives, ranging from areas that are likely to be positive, such as the creation of distributed banking networks, to less positive areas, such as how it could impact our privacy.

Blockchain and the Evolution of the Internet

Aside from being a platform for cryptocurrency, blockchain can also provide web users with the capacity to build value and verify digital information. Emerging business applications for the blockchain technology include the following:

The Sharing Industry

With new companies such as Airbnb and Uber becoming global success stories, the sharing industry is now proven as a business model. But at present, customers who like to avail of ride-sharing services have to depend on Uber as a third-party provider. But if payments can be enabled through P2P, the blockchain technology can open the door to direct transactions between the passenger and the driver, which will lead to a genuine sharing industry. One good example is the Open Bazaar, which employs blockchain to build a P2P online platform. Users can download the application on their devices, and they can easily transact with vendors without the need to pay transaction charges. The protocol implements a no rules policy, which means that personal credibility will be even more significant for these transactions compared to what is currently happening in marketplaces such as eBay.

Smart Contracts

Public ledgers allow the coding of simple contracts that will execute if the pre-set conditions are already established. One example of this is the Ethereum network, which is an open-source blockchain created especially for this purpose. Although it is still in its infancy, Ethereum has gained a lot of traction in the last few years, and cryptocurrency experts believe that it has the potential to leverage the power of blockchain on a genuine global-shaping scale.

At the present level of development of blockchain, smart contracts could be designed to perform basic functions. For example, you can pay one derivative if a financial instrument has already met a specific benchmark through the use of blockchain technology and Bitcoin which enables the automation of the payout.

Government Services

By improving the transparency and accessibility of information, blockchain technology can become a catalyst in the way government administers its basic services as well as the result of polls or elections. Smart contracts can also help to make the process faster and easier. One example is the application Boardroom, which allows organizational decisions to happen within the blockchain. This could disrupt how organizations govern and how they manage digital assets such as data and equities.

Record Keeping

A decentralized method of keeping records online will bring a lot of advantages. Disseminating data throughout the whole platform will safeguard files from getting lost or hacked. For example, the Inter-Planetary File System or IFPS makes it easy to build how a public web could function. Comparable to how BitTorrent moves data online, IPFS can eliminate the need for centralized client-server interactions such as the present form of the Internet. A new version of the World Wide Web that is composed of decentralized websites has the potential to expedite file transfer and streaming. This improvement is not only efficient but important in upgrading the Internet's presently overloaded systems for delivering content.

Intellectual Property Protection

As you might already know, there is no limit on how you can reproduce and distribute information on the Internet. This has provided many online users around the world with a huge reserve of free content. But this is not good news for holders of copyright, because they can lose control over their intellectual property. Through smart contracts, copyright can be protected. It can also automate the sale of creative content via the Web, which eliminates the risk of replication and redistribution.

One good example of this is Mycelia, which employs blockchain technology to build a P2P music distribution system. Established in the UK by the artist Imogen Heap, the platform allows artists to sell their songs directly to their fan base. It also allows artists to license samples to producers and manage royalties to musicians and songwriters. These functions work through smart contracts. This use for the blockchain has a robust chance for success because blockchain can be used to release payments in a small percentage of Bitcoin, which are also known as micropayments.

Internet of Things (IoT)

IoT refers to the network-regulated administration of specific forms of electronic devices. One example is the regulation of air temperature within a database facility. Through smart contracts, it is possible to manage the automation of remote systems. This can be done through the integration of network facilities, sensors, and software as well as the exchange of data between systems and objects. The result could improve cost monitoring as well as the efficiency of the system.

The most important players in telecommunications, tech, and manufacturing are all looking to dominate the IoT. This includes AT&T, IBM, and Samsung. An organic extension of current systems regulated by these companies, IoT apps will be able to be applied for a wide range of purposes from massive management of automated systems, data analytics, and predictive maintenance of mechanized parts.

Management of Online Identity

We have a specific requirement for improved management of our online identity. The capacity to confirm your identity is the cornerstone technology of financial transactions that could occur online. However, the resolution for the risks involved in security that come with online portals is not completely perfect. Public ledgers can provide better ways for proving who you are, alongside the possibility of digitizing personal files. Securing personal identity is also crucial for Internet communications in the sharing industry for example. Nevertheless, an outstanding reputation is the most crucial condition for conducting online transactions.

Establishing standards for digital identity can be a highly sophisticated protocol. Aside from the technical challenges, an encompassing web identity solution will require cooperation between the government as well as private organizations. The problem can be exponentially challenging if we factor in the requirement to navigate the legal systems in various countries. At present, online stores depend on the SSL certificate to ensure that the transactions online are safe.

Information Management

Using social media platforms such as Facebook and Twitter is free, right? This is not completely true. In exchange for using these platforms, you are paying these companies with your personal information. But through blockchain, you can have the capacity to administer and sell the information that their web activities produce. And because this can be easily disseminated in micro currencies, Bitcoin will be used to facilitate this transaction.

For instance, Enigma—a project in MIT—has the capacity to understand that the privacy of the user is key in creating a marketplace for personal information. It uses cryptographic strategies to allow individual information sets to be divided between nodes, and also at the same time process massive calculations over the data group in general. Scalability can be achieved by fragmenting the information, unlike in blockchain technology where information could be replicated on each node.

Stock Trading

Stock trading can also take advantage of blockchain technology through the improved efficiency of the shared platform. Once implemented, P2P trade confirmation could become more instant against the usual clearance time of 3 days. However, this could eliminate the need for custodians, auditors, and clearinghouses.

Several commodities and stock exchanges are now using early forms of blockchain technology for the services they provide. This includes the Japan Exchange Group (JPX), Frankfurt Stock Exchange (Deutsche Borse), and the Australian Securities Exchange (ASX).

Crowdfunding

Crowdfunding projects such as GoFundMe and Kickstarter are now implementing the comprehensive framework for the rising P2P economy. The popularity of these platforms signifies the increasing interest of people who want to have direct involvement in the development of specific products. Blockchain technology is elevating this interest to the next level by building venture capital funds through crowdfunding.

For example, in 2016, the Decentralized Autonomous Organization (DAO) of Ethereum managed to raise as much as $200 million within 60 days. Crowdfunders bought DAO tokens, which allow them to choose the smart contract project they are interested in. However, the project was hacked and compromised because of poor due diligence. Nonetheless, the test suggests that technology can drive new ways for people to cooperate.

The Difference Between Database and Blockchain

The difference between a blockchain and a conventional database starts with the structure or how the technology is organized. The database that runs on the World Wide Web usually uses a client-server network structure.

A registered database user who has the right permissions will be able to change the entries that are stored on a central server. In changing the master copy, each time the client is accessing a database through a device such as a computer or a smartphone, they can work on an updated version of the database entry. Database control is still within the circle of administrators, which allows for access and authorizations to be confined by a central entity.

This is not the case with blockchain. For a blockchain database, every participant could maintain, update, and compute new items within. The nodes could work together to make certain that they are all coming from the same sources, which provide built-in security for the system.

The effect of this difference is that the blockchain is well-suited as a way of recording specific functions, while a central server is completely proper for other purposes.

Basically, blockchain permits various parties that don't necessarily trust each other to access the same information without the need for authority from a centralized administration. The transactions could be processed by the users that serve as a mechanism for consensus so that everyone could create the same sharing system of record all at the same time.

The main advantage of decentralized control is that it could eliminate the risks of centralized regulation. In a centralized database, anyone with enough access level could easily corrupt or even wipe out the data. Hence, the system will highly rely on human administrators.

Many human administrators have earned enough trust that they can have full access to the database. This makes it easy for bank databases to record the money they have in their vaults. There is also a reasonable purpose for a centralized administration, and it is actually more ideal to use in special instances than blockchain technology.

However, this also means that those who need to run centralized administration have to spend substantial amounts of money to make sure that the databases will not be compromised. If the system fails, then the data could be leaked out or even stolen.

Many centralized databases are keeping information that is updated at a certain period of time. But more often than not, these are snapshots of a period that contains outdated information. On the other hand, blockchain systems are capable of keeping relevant information. Blockchain technology could create databases, which can create records of past transactions. They are capable of expanding their previous transactions into an archive while simultaneously offering real-time images.

While you can use blockchain systems to act as a records system as well as a platform for facilitating transactions, they are regarded as slow when you compare them to current technologies for digital transactions such as the technologies used by PayPal and Visa. Although it is also certain that blockchain technology will be further improved in the future, the core structure of blockchain technology calls for some speed to be left by the wayside.

The system of distributing the networks is used in blockchain so they compound and do not share processing speed and power. They each separately provide service to the whole network, and then do some comparison checks with the whole network, until the whole system agrees that the transactions are genuine. On the other hand, centralized databases are used and have been improved significantly ever since their advent in many industries.

Take note that Bitcoin is a read-uncontrolled, write-uncontrolled database. This enables everyone to add a fresh block to the ledger, which everyone could also read. An accessed-granted blockchain, similar to a centralized database could be read-controlled and write-controlled. The protocol or the network can be established so only authorized users could add new entries in the database or read the whole database.

But if trust is not an issue and confidentiality matters most, blockchain databases have no actual advantage over conventional databases with centralized administration.

Adding a concealment system to the blockchain will require complex cryptography, and this calls for more computational power for the network nodes. The best way to do this is to just completely hide the data in a private database, which does not even require connecting with the network.

CHAPTER 4

THE KING OF CRYPTOCURRENCIES: BITCOIN

Bitcoin is primarily a digital currency—a currency alternative to fiats like the U.S. dollar. It has no physical representation. It exists only on the blockchain and is commonly used as a store of value, as a hedge against inflation, for transactions, and for investments. A person's bitcoins are protected through cryptographic methods.

Satoshi Nakamoto is the founder of Bitcoin but that is all we know about him. He (if it is even proper to use that pronoun) has never even come forward to the public. (Nobody even knows if Satoshi is a person or a group of persons.)

The White Paper—the Bitcoin protocol—was issued in 2008, detailing how Bitcoin would work on the blockchain and the rules that would govern it. (Many coins have white papers, which can be thought of as a protocol—a founding document that outlines a strict set of rules for how a cryptocurrency is going to function on the blockchain.) As mentioned already, Bitcoin is the first cryptocurrency to harness the advantages of blockchain technology.

The first bitcoins were issued in 2009. The initial price for each bitcoin was less than 1 cent. However, at the end of December 2021, each bitcoin was hovering around $47,000, illustrating the exponential growth of the crypto space in general and why there is such a craze about it.

It has not always been a smooth ride though. Bitcoin's ups and downs are wild, with many people becoming financially free or bankrupt.

As implied before, Bitcoin was meant to be an alternative form of finance, free of centralized control like from the government or a corporation. No intermediary like a bank or government official is involved in any part of transactions. The only entities involved in transactions are the ones engaged in them. That is it, only the contracting parties are involved.

Bitcoin is also meant to be a hedge against inflation—protection from inflation. In order to achieve this in practical terms, the white paper stipulates that there will only ever be 21 million bitcoins in circulation. In other words, no government or central authority can devalue Bitcoin by issuing an endless supply of it, as regularly happens with the U.S. dollar.

Currently, there are 18 million bitcoins in circulation, many of which have been lost due to a myriad of reasons—something the White Paper did not seem to have foreseen. As various media reports show, some people forgot their passwords and have lost their bitcoins because they no longer have access to their digital wallets. Other people died, not having passed their bitcoins to their heirs. For such reasons, some bitcoins are forever lost from active circulation, meaning that there will never actually be 21 million bitcoins in active circulation. Fewer bitcoins in active circulation would naturally indicate that the remaining bitcoins would have even more value.

Perhaps the most illustrative example of this circumstance is Stefan Thomas, a programmer in San Francisco, who had approximately $240 million worth of bitcoins as of January 2021 locked in his digital wallet. Years before, he wrote the password to his account down on a piece of paper but lost it with no way to recover it. As of May 2021, media reports still claimed that he had two guesses left to get access to his account. If those two attempts are unsuccessful, he will lose all his bitcoins permanently.

18 million bitcoins are in circulation. The remaining—approximately 3 million—will be mined digitally. (Bitcoin mining will be covered soon.)

How Do Bitcoin Transactions Get Recorded on the Blockchain?

Each time a transaction involving Bitcoin occurs, it gets recorded in the latest block on the Bitcoin blockchain. You can think of a "block" as simply a page in Bitcoin's accounting record. A full block usually contains approximately 2,000–3,000 transactions, equaling approximately 1 MB in size.

Once a block is full, all the transactions in the block are verified, and the block is added to the chain of previous blocks; hence, the term, "blockchain." Thus, the Bitcoin blockchain is actually a complete history of all transactions that have occurred on the network ever since the very first transaction on it.

Then a new block is created for newer transactions and the process is repeated.

The list of transactions on the blockchain is publicly available. It is commonly referred to as a ledger (like an accounting ledger), and each node on the network possesses a copy of the ledger. It cannot be tampered with. As mentioned before, if anyone tries to tamper with the ledger on a node, other nodes on the network still possess the correct ledger, rendering the attempt futile.

Bitcoin as Legal Tender

What is legal tender? Legal tender essentially means that a country has accepted a currency as an officially recognized means of doing commerce. This means that businesses are obligated to accept the currency, and a person has the right to pay off debts, pay taxes, and fulfill contracts with that currency. In other words, people would be allowed to settle their financial obligations in bitcoin, that if bitcoin were to become legal tender.

If cryptocurrencies like Bitcoin are actually going to replace or compete with fiat currencies in the future as the primary means of commerce, as the founder of Bitcoin himself may have envisioned, they need to become legal tender. The average person needs to be able to use it on a day-to-day basis for day-to-day tasks like buying groceries, paying utility bills, and similar expenses.

This has not happened yet in any country—except in El Salvador. On September 7, 2021, El Salvador became the first country in the world to accept Bitcoin as legal tender. Beyond this, a massive developmental project called the Bitcoin Beach Initiative is being implemented in the country in a small coastal town called El Zonte. A massive, anonymous donation of Bitcoin dedicated to this project is being used to fund these developmental initiatives. Locals are using Bitcoin for a variety of everyday transactions like buying groceries, accepting salaries, and paying utility bills.

Such initiatives in El Salvador are a major milestone in the cryptocurrency space's history. What was once a dream and then a fringe idea gained growing acceptance and has now become the legal tender of a sovereign state.

It begs the question: Which country is next? Is this just the first step toward the worldwide adoption of cryptocurrencies as legal tender in almost every country? These are questions that indicate the real possibility of such an occurrence, even if they occur decades from now.

The Challenges Facing Bitcoin

Bitcoin is about to become 1 decade-old digital currency, but it has still a long way before it can be accepted by the general public. As a matter of fact, the challenges that this cryptocurrency is facing today are quite the same that it experienced when it was still in its introductory phase.

When Bitcoin was first released, the primary hindrance was the computer skills and understanding of the blockchain jargon required to scrutinize the platform itself. This revolutionary technology involves solving complex algorithms for the verification of transactions, which was quite difficult for a layman to chew.

Since then, Bitcoin's disruptive features made it enticing for users of the underground market or those who are using the Dark Web. Bitcoin became a popular currency for illegal transactions such as criminal activities like drug deals and money laundering.

As a result, Bitcoin was placed in a bad light, which was worsened by the fact that it can be difficult for government agencies and financial authorities to monitor the transactions in Bitcoin's blockchain. While some governments such as China have issued an outright ban on Bitcoins, other governments such as Japan and the United States still made their due diligence to understand how this cryptocurrency works.

The price volatility also added another layer of challenge for people to accept Bitcoin as payment. In order for widespread adoption to occur, Bitcoins should be stable, should be usable, and should be easily accessible by the general public.

Some advocates believe that there must be changes in the Bitcoin ecosystem in order to capture the mainstream users. For once, the concept should be simplified to earn the public's trust and interest. At present, around 90% of the global population is still not aware of the existence of Bitcoin.

Why Hackers Are Using Bitcoin

Just recently, the series of attacks on private serves has stirred again a long-time discussion on the vulnerabilities of virtual currencies. Just in case you are still not aware, dangerous malware has been released and spread over 150 countries around the world. The mechanism of the ransomware attack was quite simple. A personal computer will be infected with a virus, which will encrypt files until the owner pays a certain amount as ransom.

In the recent attacks, the people behind the ransomware are asking victims to pay $300 in Bitcoins. And it doesn't end there. If the victim does not pay after 3 days, the ransom will be doubled, and after 7 days and no payment has been received, all the files will be deleted from the computers.

Meanwhile, there is no actual guarantee that the files will be restored again and will be safe if the victim pays the ransom.

The involvement of Bitcoin as a mode of paying the ransom again placed this digital currency in a bad light. It becomes an easy tool for hackers because of its special features as a virtual currency. In sending money over digital channels, you can either use your credit cards or online banking, which is linked to your personal information such as your name and address.

But this is not the case with Bitcoin. All the dealings you make via this currency can be concealed. Remember, when you choose to trade in BTCs, a private key that is linked to your wallet will be used to create an encrypted code. This code will be publicly linked with the transaction but not with the people behind the dealings.

Hence, each deal is recorded in a public ledger, which anyone could access and check. Security experts believe that among the possible reasons why hackers and cybercriminals are using BTC as a mode of payment is because it is designed to conceal identity.

In the past, hackers preferred PayPal for their unscrupulous transactions, but because of stricter guidelines in using an online platform such as PayPal, they now prefer Bitcoins.

CHAPTER 5

The Queen of Cryptocurrencies: Ethereum

After Bitcoin, Ethereum is the second-largest cryptocurrency by market cap, although, by December 2021, it had not even reached 40% of Bitcoin's size. (Once again, this illustrates the dominance of Bitcoin in the cryptocurrency space.)

However, Ethereum is a beastly creature in its own right.

Its price has been growing much faster than Bitcoin's since the market crash in 2020. An investment in Ethereum has been several times more lucrative than an identical investment in Bitcoin during that same timeframe. A glance at Ethereum's 2-year chart compared with Bitcoin's 2-year chart would make this claim obvious.

Many people are speculating that because of Ethereum's far greater number of real-world use-cases compared with Bitcoin's (as will be shown later), Ethereum's market cap will continue to outpace Bitcoin's growth for the foreseeable future until Ethereum eventually surpasses Bitcoin. Perhaps this could happen within the next decade or even sooner. As such, some people believe that Ethereum will eventually replace Bitcoin as the leader of the cryptocurrency space.

Then there would be no need to call Ethereum an altcoin anymore.

Many people perhaps do not know the distinction between Ethereum and ether, so it is important to make that distinction clear before continuing on. Ethereum is essentially a platform for the Ethereum network and programs. Ether, on the other hand, is the Ethereum network's native cryptocurrency. It has myriad uses—investments, store of value to combat inflation, Ethereum programs, and commerce within and outside of the platform.

Ethereum is clearly making inroads into mainstream finance. Large banks like Goldman Sachs and Morgan Stanley are now offering select clients exposure to ether, just as they have provided exposure to Bitcoin.

This chapter will provide a foundational understanding of Ethereum and its most prominent aspects like NFTs and DeFi. With the knowledge contained herein, you will not be like a lost sheep anymore when you try to read or watch the information about Ethereum. You will be able to follow along, even if you have to do additional research at times to keep up.

With that said, Ethereum is conceptually much broader than Bitcoin. And it is constantly growing and evolving, as will be shown in this chapter and the next. As such, gaining a deeper understanding of Ethereum will require much more time and effort, but at least this chapter will give you the basic tools.

If you are interested to delve deeper into Ethereum, its website (ethereum.org) is the ideal place to start. In addition, plenty of helpful tutorials are also available on YouTube that can provide a comprehensive understanding of every aspect of the platform.

What Is Ethereum?

Let us begin with the basics: Ethereum was founded in 2013 by Vitalik Buterin. (The white paper—the founding document—is available on Ethereum's website.)

Ether began to trade in 2015, 6 years after Bitcoin. As such, Bitcoin had the first-mover advantage by approximately 6 years, but as mentioned earlier, Ethereum is, at times, fast closing the gap in terms of market capitalization.

As its website claims, Ethereum builds on the idea of Bitcoin, which is the idea of a digital currency. In other words, while Bitcoin is primarily digital money, Ethereum is also that, but much more.

So, what is Ethereum? Ethereum is essentially a vast, decentralized blockchain network that hosts a variety of computer programs called "decentralized applications" ("dApps" for short). (The term, "dApps" is commonly used in crypto media.) Essentially, these dApps are "apps"—a term that most people would be familiar with.

Ethereum is thus a kind of mini-Internet, a marketplace, a kind of virtual mall, where people create and use a whole suite of dApps, for all kinds of purposes like gaming, finance, and insurance. That is why Ethereum's founders refer to it as a "programmable blockchain." (Developers use a programming language called solidity to write code and create dApps.)

When reading about the Ethereum blockchain, one comes across the term "smart contracts." The term smart contracts is just a more complicated term for these dApps.

The question that comes to mind is: How are these dApps different from apps that you might find on your phone, for example? The main difference is that dApps on the blockchain function without any human oversight or centralized control. They are self-automated and self-executing, as will be explained shortly.

The Ethereum website gives a simple example to illustrate the concept: Smart contracts are like vending machines—put coins into a vending slot, and the machine will automatically do the work for you. It will figure out your selection, calculate the amount on its own, and then use a bunch of levers to dispense the snack. The functioning is automatic and has no human intervention at all, except for you making your initial selection of a snack.

Thus, when you use an Ethereum application, you are basically using a program that is as automatic and self-executing as a vending machine. You can trust that no human oversight or intervention is possible. The rules for the smart contract cannot be altered or tampered with, such as by a government or corporate official. In other words, the code is permanent and unalterable once the dApp is uploaded.

For example, if someone executes a trade on a decentralized exchange, the trade cannot be reversed by any human oversight or tampered with in any way. Market makers cannot bend the rules and halt trading whenever they wish (the way Robinhood did during the GameStop short squeeze in 2021).

Thus, dApps give new meaning to the freedom of the individual in a variety of realms. (dApps will be explained in greater detail in the section below.) Just as with Bitcoin, the individual is freer from centralized control—be it government or corporate.

More on Smart Contracts

The Ethereum website sorts its smart contract platform into three categories: decentralized finance (DeFi), non-fungible tokens (NFTs), and decentralized autonomous organizations (DAOs).

An understanding of these three categories gives one a basic framework for what Ethereum offers, an appreciation of its potential, and how it significantly builds on Bitcoin's initial innovation of a digital currency using blockchain technology.

This section will provide an overview of each of the categories mentioned above.

The first category is called "decentralized finance," also known by the popular abbreviation "DeFi." DeFi is the rage today, perhaps the most-watched sector of cryptocurrencies. If you watch videos about cryptocurrency on YouTube regularly or follow a crypto-related publication, chances are that you have heard about DeFi plenty of times.

Ethereum's DeFi is a massive platform for dApps that provide financial services. Through these dApps, you can invest, borrow, lend, collect interest, and more. Billions of dollars flow through the platform. It is clearly intended to be a complete financial system—one that may even rival Wall Street one day in terms of size and scope.

Now that is a bold statement.

In addition, through DeFi, you can even mint new cryptocurrencies. These cryptocurrencies operate on the Ethereum network and are called ERC-20 tokens, meaning that they depend on the Ethereum network to function and adhere to certain standard rules in their code. Some of these tokens—like Tether and Chainlink—have even developed into behemoths themselves, becoming some of the largest cryptocurrencies by market cap.

Many other ERC-20 tokens are soaring in market cap, and the growth of these coins contributes to the prominence and indispensability of the Ethereum platform as a gargantuan financial hub.

But the main difference between mainstream finance and DeFi is that DeFi has no market makers, no intermediaries, and nobody to "oversee" a transaction or take a slice from you. The system is self-executing and always follows the same rules embedded in the code.

Thus, as mentioned in the last section, nobody can take arbitrary action and freeze trading, as happened during the GameStop short squeeze in early 2021—actions that tremendously benefit the ultra-rich at the expense of everyone else. Also, unlike in traditional finance, markets are always open in DeFi and transactions are always final and irreversible.

As opposed to traditional banks and financial institutions, with DeFi you do not even have to provide your personal data or open a bank account. Thus, privacy in finance is taking on a new meaning. All you need to do is open an Ethereum wallet and get some ether in it. That is all.

The benefit of this is huge for many people. Many millions of people across the world, who do not have access to a bank account or who are reluctant to provide their personal data to banks, can use these services without giving up their personal identities.

Apart from these benefits, there are other revolutionary benefits as well that can significantly improve day-to-day commerce for everyone: people, corporations, and even governments, whether it be moving minuscule or large funds around.

Because DeFi is automated, the technology ensures that transactions are quicker, more efficient, and cheaper. Money can be sent around the world within seconds, if not instantly, unlike in traditional finance, where this can take days.

For all the above reasons, DeFi is a promising and thriving space. It has gotten investors excited about future prospects for growth (as evidenced by the rocketing price of Ethereum over the past one and a half years). As mentioned, billions of dollars flow through these dApps on DeFi. From 2019 to 2021 alone, the amount of money flowing through these dApps has increased from approximately $1 billion to about $80 billion,18 representing an 80-fold increase in just 2 years.

As more people use Ethereum, it is easy to imagine that this technology will continue to become much larger and a more viable alternative global financial system in the next decade.

Decentralized Autonomous Organizations (DAOs)

NFT artwork and DeFi are the most prominent faces of Ethereum. Decentralized autonomous organizations (or DAOs, for short) are perhaps the least well-known part of Ethereum. But this could also mean that it has a high upside for potential adoption.

DAOs are essentially digital organizations or cooperatives on the blockchain. Just like real-world organizations, they are diverse and wide-ranging. They can be corporations, not-for-profits, crowd-funding organizations, etc., catering to a wide range of purposes from venture capitalism to charity.

Because DAOs are smart contracts, the rules of an organization are already programmed into the code of the organization. Thus, just like other smart contracts, how the organization functions is a self-executing process.

Thus, it is not within any member's discretion to change the rules at will. If anyone wants to change the rules of how an organization works, they must bring it up with the organization as a whole. The other members vote on the proposed rule change. Everyone has an equal vote. If the vote is favorable, a change in the code is made.

The same is true when an organization needs to make a decision. A member makes a proposal, a discussion or debate takes place between all members, and then a vote is held. All members have an equal vote. Once a decision has been made, the decision is implemented through code.

In this way, DAOs are democratic in spirit and practice, seeking to infuse these ideals in organizations across the world. DAOs seek to eliminate centralized control and hierarchy (like a CEO or board of directors), as found in traditional corporate and political governance structures.

Although the space is relatively new, it has already seen a wide range of organizations adopt the Ethereum platform. For example, people of color are using DAOs to share their life experiences and stories. HerStoryDao is an example of this; an art collective showcasing NFT artwork by black women. There are non-traditional venture capitalist DAOs as well, such as MetaCartel, which invests in start-up dApps.

The point is that DAO growth on the Ethereum platform has the potential to be exponential if people see it as an attractive avenue to establish organizations. If more existing businesses and organizations use it, this area can multiply Ethereum's usage, and hence, growth manifold.

CHAPTER 6

MOST COMMONLY USED CRYPTOCURRENCIES

Since bitcoin has been presented, various progressed money-related structures have entered the market. Different elective cryptographic sorts of money or altcoins have been dispatched—following the achievement of Bitcoin, and they have been shaped by many others. Some are being sold more reasonably than Bitcoin, while some will, generally speaking, be more open than Bitcoin. In this piece of the book, 12 of the most standard cryptographic kinds of money will be told. Perhaps you as of late got some answers concerning Bitcoin and have some puzzling things about how it works, yet this time you will enter the universe of cryptocurrency and see what the exciting monetary standards are inside cryptographic money.

Bitcoin (BTC)

Bitcoin is the first and most standard cryptographic money on earth; some don't consider its reality yet it genuinely remains as an overall segment framework. Bitcoin has no bank; truly, it depends upon numerical confirmations. Additionally, with the improvement of e-mail, nobody has controlled the arrangement of Bitcoin. Without a doubt, even the party and individual behind it truly stays a mystery, just the pseudonym Nakamoto has been acquainted with everyone.

To have a Bitcoin you need to seek after an online wallet first. Truly, a virtual wallet for virtual cash. There are kinds of online wallets you can pursue, and they're completely allowed to utilize. Next is to purchase a bitcoin from others utilizing business centers around the web; regardless, you can additionally utilize mechanized cash exchanges like Kraken, CEX.IO, Coinbase, Bitstamp, and BitFinex. Most exchanger needs to relate any of your cards or records to make a buy. You would now have the alternative to go to the trade's purchase district and select the extent of bitcoin you need to purchase. Bitcoin changes its inspiration here and there, it can increase or diminish respect—nobody knows. Bitcoin has a transparently accessible report called "blockchain," which fills in as a record for each Bitcoin exchange. The blockchain has a making outline record considered blocks that are validated by cryptography; when the block has been recorded it can't be changed any longer.

Bitcoin can be utilized in buying stock, sending cash, travel setting up for the web, and purchasing mechanized things. By this, exchanges are made with no centerman, which suggests no banks are required to fit as a fiddle or structure.

Ethereum (ETH)

In 2011, a software engineer named Vitalik Buterin from Toronto first developed an interest in Bitcoin. Buterin, a 19-year-old around then has assisted with building up the online news site Bitcoin Magazine and made a couple of articles about the cryptocurrency world. In the year 2013, Buterin passed on the white paper. What portrays an elective stage got ready for any decentralized application an architect needs to manufacture. The design was then called Ethereum. Comparably, like Bitcoin, Ethereum is in like the way a dissipated public blockchain network. Even though there is some particular separation between the two cryptographic money because, in Ethereum, miners work to get Ether as opposed to mining. Ether is a digit of code that permits the program or application to run—nobody has Ethereum, regardless, its construction supporting its capacity isn't free. Not in the least like Bitcoin, Ether doesn't have a cap limit, indeed, 13 million Ether are mined every year.

To purchase an Ether, you need to discover it on the web or an individual who has it and simultaneously needs to exchange it for cash. There is additionally another choice on the off chance that you need to have an Ether available, some undertaking to buy a bitcoin first from trusted bitcoin exchangers by then exchange it for Ethereum.

Litecoin (LTC)

This electronic cash is comparably conveyed by mining; it was made by Google's previous organizer Charles Lee in October 2011. Litecoin is made to improve the speed of mining from the bound period of 10 minutes to 2.5 minutes while conveying a block. The said online cash has a quicker exchange than Bitcoin because it utilizes "content calculation," which favors a titanic extent of fast RAM that is the clarification content known as the "memory inconvenient issue." Also, like Bitcoin, Litecoin has additionally its restriction of 84 million coins and a market cap of $540, 274,528.26.

- Litecoin can deal with a high volume of exchanges.

- Reduces two-fold spending assault.

- Fast affirmation particularly for traders.

Ripple (XRP)

Is Ripple comparable to Bitcoin? Considering everything, it's a huge NO. Ripple is a money trade and reimbursement network that utilizes a common record managed by affiliation and is supported by free workers. The Ripple Labs, a general cash exchange firm that is past OpenCoin, was helped with development by CEO Chris Larsen and CTO Jed McCaleb who is a ton of ground in motorized money. Jed McCaleb is at present dealing with the common piece of Bitcoin exchanges in the world. While Larsen used to be the great partner of the money-related affiliation E-LOAN—the remainder of the Ripple plans, in addition, consider Bitcoin. Ripple depends upon a common public data set, a huge separation from Bitcoin that is made by energy and taking care of raised proof of work. Ripple doesn't utilize blockchain progression, the affiliation will likely keep the cash streaming transparently.

Dash (DASH)

Dash was first dispatched as Xcoin, by then changed its name into Darkcoin, and in 2015 the Darkcoin has been rebranded into Dash, which is as of now the sixth most unmistakable cryptocurrency on earth. Dash is a scattered cryptocurrency that was forked out from Bitcoin bringing it into quicker and more private exchanges. Dash is quick to have a decentralized blockchain association framework, also as different automated kinds of money. Dash is, in addition, trying to understand a piece of Bitcoin's loads. It gives speedier exchanges and more dark assistance to its clients. Dash exchanges are made inside 4 seconds, a long way from the exchange example of Bitcoin that routinely requires 10 minutes to wrap up. Dash is additionally procured by mining, comparably to Bitcoin.

Monero (XMR)

Monero is progressed cash that has the most secret when it goes to its exchanges made. It is a gotten and untraceable cash framework that utilizes an excellent sort of cryptography for a 100% unlikeable exchange. Monero gets a basic level of undeniable quality because of its security coordinated highlights after it was dispatched in 2014. The mining cycle utilized by Monero depends upon the Egalitarian idea.

IOTA (MIOTA)

The cryptographic money IOTA is a ton not by and large identical to the dominating piece of online monetary rules—it's gotten ready for machine yet can't be mined. IOTA connotes "Web of Things Application," which watches out for the versatility issues of blockchain and the exchange expenses simultaneously by disposing of the square and chain. The experts are to just check two past exchanges, to submit them to the IOTA record. The absolute flexibility of these coins are fixed into 2,779,530,283,277,761 coins. Farm trucks don't need to control the affiliation and there is no focal record for this high-level cash.

Zcash (ZEC)

Zcash is dispatched by Roger Ver, Barry Seibert, and the

Pantera Capital on October 28, 2016. Zcash is a decentralized and open-source automated money that utilizes an astounding guarantee about an affiliation called "zk-snark." This remarkable part permits the relationship to keep up and secure the record without uncovering the sums in each exchange.

Stellar (XLM)

Jed McCaleb, the wonderful partner of Ripple, is the maker of this Stellar Cryptocurrency, which is comparatively a bit advancement. Stellar is practically tantamount to the accompanying part improvements—a decentralized worker runs the relationship with a spread record, then is strengthened each 2 to 5 seconds. It doesn't just rely on miners, but rather utilizes Federated Byzantine Agreement (FBA) algorithm, which helps for a speedier exchange.

NEM (XEM)

NEM was dispatched on March 31, 2015, as a typical cryptocurrency and blockchain stage, written in Java and C++ programming language. NEM means "New Economy Movement," not in any manner like most exceptional money-related norms NEM has its own game plan figuring. This can upset assaults against the affiliation and every one of the trades made. NEM expects to make a sharp resource blockchain that can perform critical overabundance occupations that should be finished.

NEO (NEO)

NEO is the chief decentralized and open-source cryptocurrency in China, which was set up by Da Hongfei. Neo is a cryptocurrency and blockchain stage simultaneously, it was dispatched in 2014 as "Antshares" and debranded in June 2017 as "NEO." NEO can keep 10,000 exchanges for each second, utilizing the Byzantine Fault Tolerance (Daft) game plan structure.

TRON (TRX)

This cryptographic money was first presented on September 9, 2017, and was set up by the TRON Foundation—a non-advantage relationship from Singapore. TRON is in like the way a decentralized uninhibitedly conveyed progressed cash, at any rate, has a part of an application. TRONs improvement is a storeroom that awards clients admittance to content taking everything together into pieces of the world, with no help from Google Play Store. It besides permits content makers to acquire from sharing their substance.

CHAPTER 7

THE RISING STARS: SOLANA, POLKADOT, AND BINANCE COIN

While it would be impossible to discuss every single cryptocurrency out there, it is important to at least provide a brief synopsis of a few other prominent projects as well that could become as large as Bitcoin and Ethereum themselves in the distant future.

A very bold claim indeed. But no promises. And nothing in this book should be interpreted as financial advice.

The currencies that will be discussed in this chapter are Solana, Polkadot, and Binance Coin. Each of these projects offers something unique and will give you an idea of the way that people are harnessing blockchain technology to proffer different, creative digital solutions. The crypto space is indeed a bustling and innovative one.

These particular coins have been selected because of their rapid rise in 2020 and 2021 and because they are some of the largest cryptocurrencies after Bitcoin in terms of market capitalization. (That does not mean that other projects are not just as promising or even more. In this sense, the selections in this chapter may be somewhat arbitrary.) You may have already heard about these coins on YouTube, but do not really know anything about them beyond their names.

Before analyzing each of the above-mentioned coins, an observation will be made: it is evident that smart contract platforms have been on the rise, especially during the past 2 years. Some of these platforms seem to be building off of Ethereum's vision and offering their own unique innovations, while Ethereum in turn seems to be rebuilding itself with Ethereum 2.0 to outdo its competition.

After Bitcoin, the largest cryptocurrencies by market cap, as of January 2022 are Ethereum, Tether, Solana, Cardano, and Polkadot. All—except Tether—are smart contract platforms. (Even Bitcoin has smart contract capabilities, though this function is not nearly as large as Ethereum's.) Apart from Bitcoin and Ethereum, none of these cryptocurrencies were even in the top 5 12 months ago, demonstrating the dramatic rise of smart contract platforms since the market crash in 2020. (You can view each of their price charts on CoinMarketCap.com to verify this claim.)

Smart contract platforms are probably the future of cryptocurrencies. So, why are they on the rise as opposed to other cryptocurrencies modeled after Bitcoin, such as Bitcoin Cash or Litecoin? The answer is obvious: Smart contract platforms provide many more practical, real-world use cases compared to platforms like Bitcoin and Litecoin which are mainly or exclusively digital currencies. They offer what Bitcoin offers (an alternative to fiat currency) and significantly more.

A brief description of each currency mentioned in this chapter's title will now be provided. It will become immediately apparent that each platform described below essentially offers some sort of improvement or innovation over Ethereum 1.0.

Solana (SOL)

The Solana Foundation, which is based in Switzerland, created the cryptocurrency Solana (ticker symbol: SOL).

Solana's success has been jaw-dropping thus far, and an analysis of the platform would give a person a good reason to speculate that the future is still bright for it. (This does not mean that the road ahead will not be bumpy at times.)

A $1,000 investment in Solana in December 2020 would have grown to roughly $225,000 by November 2021. (These calculations can be confirmed through Solana's price action chart.) Even by cryptocurrency standards, these are impressive gains and certainly more lucrative than an investment in either Bitcoin or Ethereum during the same timeframe. Such investments are, of course, far riskier as well and much more difficult to predict.

So, what is Solana, and what does it offer? Similar to Ethereum, Solana is a smart contract platform and already hosts an array of services for both DeFi and NFTs.

However, it is much faster, more efficient, cheaper, and more environmentally friendly than Ethereum 1.0. While Ethereum 1.0 can process around 15 transactions per second, Solana can process approximately 65,000 transactions per second, with plans to scale up even more than that. It boasts the fastest payment system in the world, making it faster than even Visa—the second-fastest in the world.

Solana is much less energy and resource-intensive than the current version of Ethereum because it relies on the proof-of-stake method.

The network is extremely cheap to use—just a fraction of a cent per transaction, whereas Ethereum 1.0 currently has high gas fees, as already mentioned. So, it is easy to understand why Solana has shot up thus far: It is the fastest network in the world and possibly the cheapest one as well.

To achieve higher transaction speeds while maintaining extremely low costs, Solana uses, in addition to the proof-of-stake method, a method called proof-of-history. This combination is unique to Solana. Essentially, the proof-of-history method is a way of having a validator (computer on the network) individually time-stamp transactions as they are being recorded in a block.

So, how does this method further increase Solana's transaction speed? Basically, nodes on other networks like Bitcoin and Ethereum spend time and energy with each other to figure out the order and time of transactions. To bypass this wasteful chatter between different nodes, a validator on Solana is essentially able to independently and accurately time-stamp transactions and process them quickly without the need to communicate with other nodes.

The results have been astounding thus far: Solana is fast-growing, especially in DeFi. Developers have already built hundreds of dApps in the DeFi space already. Furthermore, their website claims that Solana's DeFi and NFT space is the fastest growing in the world. Billions of dollars have already flowed through these dApps.

Due to all of this growth and the overall platform's speed, efficiency, and low transaction costs, Solana has been dubbed as one of the "eth killers,"—a reference to Ethereum—because some people predict that Solana will eventually overtake Ethereum in market cap in the long term as the number one platform for smart contracts, the way some people view Ethereum as overtaking Bitcoin one day as the largest cryptocurrency by market cap.

However, replacing Ethereum would be a difficult task and would probably take many painstaking years to occur (if it were to do so at all). Ethereum is already significantly more well-established than Solana. It is the global leader in smart contracts—the Apple or Google of cryptocurrencies. Overthrowing such a behemoth is a florid claim, easier said than done. Ethereum has many more apps, many times more nodes, and significantly greater commerce on its platform.

Moreover, Ethereum is already going ahead with 2.0 upgrades, making the chances for Solana to overtake Ethereum even more difficult. Nevertheless, for the reasons mentioned above, if a cryptocurrency were to overtake Ethereum, Solana would be one of the prime candidates to do so.

Polkadot (DOT)

The Web 3.0 Foundation, based in Switzerland, created the Polkadot project, which is essentially the Polkadot cryptocurrency (ticker: DOT) and platform.

Polkadot began to trade in 2017. Since then, its price has risen multifold, particularly since 2020. A $1,000 investment in mid-2020 could have grown to approximately $9,000 by mid-2021. Not as great as Solana's explosive movements during the same timeframe, but enough to catapult Polkadot to within the top 5 cryptocurrencies by market cap by October 2021.

So, what is Polkadot, and what is unique about it?

Polkadot is a network of blockchains connected to the main chain, called the "Relay Chain." In other words, Polkadot is a whole ecosystem of interconnected blockchains, each chain performing its own tasks, sharing data with other chains in a fast, efficient, and seamless manner.

These blockchains are called parachains and parathreads. A project can purchase a parachain on lease for approximately 2 years to gain access to the Polkadot network. Parathreads, on the other hand, are "pay-as-you-go" blockchains, which are a cheaper option for projects that do not have sufficient capital to lease a whole parachain.

Polkadot also has the capacity to connect with external blockchains, such as Ethereum and Bitcoin through a process called "bridging." Bridging allows the connected blockchains to share data with each other. These bridges are mutually beneficial for both Polkadot and for external blockchains. For example, a bridge with Ethereum gives Polkadot users access to ERC-20 tokens and Ethereum's smart contracts.

Polkadot's multichain system of blockchains is a significant innovation in the cryptocurrency space. This multichain system distributes tasks among interconnected blockchains, thus increasing the speed and efficiency of the Polkadot network as a whole. Other cryptocurrencies, on the other hand, usually function on singular blockchains. For example, Ethereum 1.0 functions on a single blockchain. This is less efficient than Polkadot's system because all tasks and transactions burden a single Ethereum blockchain.

Polkadot's multichain structure is meant to be a transition toward Web 3.0, which is the idea of a decentralized internet—an internet that is run by a network of blockchains, as opposed to through a bunch of central servers.

To elaborate, the structure of Web 3.0 is different from the more centralized structures of Web 2.0, which is the current version of the Internet and is dominated by tech giants like Google, Microsoft, Facebook, and Apple. Proponents of Web 3.0 criticize Web 2.0 for being too centralized, in the hands of tech giants that collect hordes of personal data and store them in massive servers as large as sports arenas.

The problem, they argue, is that the freedom of the individual is compromised in this system. Tech giants not only collect personal data but also sometimes sell them illegally to third-party entities for a profit, as Facebook has famously done.

The human being in this system is a lucrative target, exploited for massive corporate profit, and is continuously bombarded with algorithms designed to keep people addicted to their devices, therefore, personal data is incessantly collected for perpetual corporate profit. It's a kind of enslavement with all kinds of unsavory repercussions such as mental health, for example.

Polkadot's mission is to create a new, decentralized internet in which the agency of the individual is restored, in which your data is not used as a tool for corporate profit. So, Polkadot can be thought of as striving to be the early beginnings of Web 3.0.

Binance Coin (BNB)

To understand Binance Coin (ticker symbol: BNB), it is important to understand Binance. By June 2021, it became the largest cryptocurrency exchange platform in the world, offering approximately 500 different coins for trading. It was founded in 2017 and is currently headquartered in the Cayman Islands.

Ever since its inception, Binance has faced legal troubles, first in China (which clamped down on Binance's business activities due to the Chinese government's efforts to tamp down on cryptocurrencies in general) and then eventually in the US and UK, where it has been under investigation due to fraud and embezzlement charges. (It is important to note that Binance is different from Binance US. The latter was established in the US in place of the former because of Binance's legal troubles in the US.)

However, as indicated above, these issues have not prevented Binance's meteoric rise in the cryptocurrency space. As of November 2021, Binance Coin has reached the fourth largest market cap in the cryptocurrency space. And its future seems bright: The network is speedy, having the capability to settle approximately 1.4 million transactions per second.

Binance Coin is the native token for Binance's two blockchains—Binance Chain and Binance Smart Chain. Binance Chain was created in April 2019. To improve the network, Binance then added the second chain, Binance Smart Chain, in 2020. Both chains are "interoperable," meaning that they work together in sharing data and information seamlessly, quickly, and efficiently.

The reason that the second chain was added was to increase the speed and performance of the network and to improve smart contract functionality. Ethereum smart contracts can also function on Binance Smart Chain—a key feature and attraction for the upgrade.

Binance Coin is also a utility token. This means that you can use the token for a range of special benefits, whether within the Binance ecosystem itself (such as in Binance Dex) or with external partners. For example, Binance Coin users can get cheaper transaction costs in the Binance network, and they can get special access to travel accommodations or get a loan from Binance partners.

A prominent feature of Binance Coin is how it tackles inflation: Other cryptocurrencies like Bitcoin have a fixed number of coins in circulation. No one—such as a central bank—can arbitrarily increase this number, and thus decrease the value of each Bitcoin.

But Binance goes even further than that: Every quarter, it uses one-fifth of its profits to buy back coins and "burn them," which is deleting them from circulation, thus reducing the total number of Binance coins in circulation each quarter. Such reduction of supply naturally increases demand, and hence, the value of each Binance coin. So far, Binance has eliminated $649,462,868 worth of coins as of the third quarter of 2021. The goal is to reach a total supply of 1 million total coins in circulation—down from the original 2 million coins in 2017.

Binance uses a proof-of-stake authority system to validate transactions. This is a combination of proof of stake and proof of authority. (Proof of stake has already been explained in the section on Ethereum.)

Proof of authority is essentially a system whereby only 21 validators are selected from the entire network to confirm blocks of transactions. These 21 validators, updated daily, possess the highest number of Binance coins in the network. The idea is to limit the number of validators on the network.

Another way the exchange tries to combat inflation is by rewarding validators in the network with existing Binance coins—not by minting new ones.

The fact that Binance has its own coin, which has now become the fourth-largest cryptocurrency by market cap, naturally leads one to speculate whether other exchanges such as Coinbase and Kraken will eventually create their own coins. If this happens, then will minting digital coins for exchanges be a trend in the future of cryptocurrencies? It is hard to imagine that such will not be the case.

CHAPTER 8

Advantages and Disadvantages of Cryptocurrencies

Advantages

Some other advantages of cryptocurrency trading can be seen below:

Transactions

The otherwise easy deal may be made costlier by conventional company contracts, traders, marketers, and legal representatives. Paperwork, brokerage fees, commissions, and any other special terms can apply.

One of the benefits of blockchain trading is that it is one-on-one, a peer-to-peer networking structure that traditional practices are "cutting the middle man off." This makes audit tracks simpler, less ambiguous on who is to pay whom, and more accountable since each of the two parties involved in a deal knows who they are.

Asset Transfers

One financial specialist defines the cryptocurrency blockchain as equivalent to a "massive property rights ledger," which can be used to introduce and implement contracts with two-party parties for commodity goods such as cars or property. However, the cryptocurrency ecosystem blockchain may also be used to promote professional transition processes.

Cryptocurrency contracts may, for example, be structured to complement third-party permissions, to mention external evidence, or to be settled in the future at some time or date defined. And because you—as the owners of cryptocurrency—rule your account entirely, this minimizes time and cost in allowing transactions of properties.

More Confidential Transactions

Each time you make an exchange for the cash/credit schemes, the entire transaction history will become a bank/credit agency reference record. At the most straightforward stage, it can require checking your account's balance to make sure enough money is given. For more complex or business-critical transactions, a complete review of the financial record may be sufficient.

Another critical benefit of cryptocurrencies is that any deal you do is a single exchange of terms and conditions between two parties. Furthermore, information sharing takes place "press" to relay specifically what you intend to give to the receiver—and nothing more.

This safeguards your financial past privacy and prohibits you from being revealed at some point in the transaction chain by a more considerable danger to account or identification amount in the conventional system.

Transaction Fees

You have read the monthly bank or credit card business account statements and have balked at the volume of the payment charges levied for checks, moving cash, or breathing in the face of the banking firms concerned. Transaction charges can take a big bite from your savings—especially if you carry out several transactions in a month.

Fees from crypto-currency networks typically do not extend because the data miners (remarkable and different computer systems) who crunch the number created by bitcoin earn compensation. Bitcoin and other cryptocurrencies

Greater Access to Credit

Cryptocurrencies are enabled by automated data transmission and the Internet. These services are also feasible for anybody who has a viable data connection, a specific knowledge of the provided cryptocurrency networks, and ready access to their respective websites and portals.

There are figures that globally, 2,2 billion people now have Internet or telephone connectivity but do not currently have access to conventional banking and exchange networks. This massive market of eager customers—if the appropriate infrastructure (digital and regulatory) is placed together—can embrace cryptocurrency ecosystems to allow wealth transactions and transaction processing available.

Easier International Trade

While currently largely unregulated as a legal tender at the national level, it is by their very existence that cryptocurrencies are not subject to a particular country's exchange rates, interest rates, transaction costs, and any extra fees.

Cross-border exchanges and transactions can be carried out without risks of currency volatility, etc., using the peer-to-peer system of blockchain technology.

Individual Ownership

You turn the administration of your finances over in a conventional bank or credit card scheme to a third party who conducts life or death over your money. Accounts can be suspended without warning for infringements of a financial company's terms of operation—forcing you as a manager of the store to leap through hoops to add to the scheme.

Maybe the main benefit in the case of cryptocurrencies is that you alone possess the associated private and public cryptocurrency keys to shape the identification or address of your cryptocurrency network unless you have assigned the control of your wallet to the third-party provider.

Adaptability

More than 13,400 separate cryptocurrencies and altcoins are already in worldwide circulation. Many of them are somewhat brief, but importantly, cryptocurrencies' versatility is demonstrated in real use cases.

There are, for example, "privacy coins" to cover up the identity on the blockchain and supply chain tokens to allow supply chain processes for different types of industries.

Strong Security

Since the sale of a cryptocurrency is accepted, it cannot be revoked, as in credit card companies' "chargeback" purchases. This is a precaution against theft, forcing the customer and vendor to agree on refunds in the case of an error or return policies.

The robust encryption methods used in the distributed ledger (blockchain) and transaction processes in cryptocurrencies secure against theft and account abuse and maintain customer confidentiality.

Better Payment Structure

You will want to explore crypto use if you have ever been angry waiting for a cash transfer from a bank account. Instant payments are less costly than services such as PayPal. The use of crypto also prevents illegitimate charges, and transfers cannot be reversed on a blockchain.

You can also transfer money anywhere you want using crypto without any broker checking your transaction history. This requires foreign beneficiaries who willingly stop the costly currency exchange costs of PayPal.

Another benefit when using blockchain is the idea of micropayment or an on-demand payment structure. The embedded fees you pay with a credit card vanish with blockchain, making micropayments a fact every second or minute. Instead of paying a streaming video subscription fee, you can pay crypto for watching a movie, for example. Streamium is also a video streaming service that accepts crypto.

Growth Investment

Even if you are not an enormous crypto buff, you undoubtedly heard about Bitcoin's mania around Christmas 2017. Bitcoin soared in terms of valuation, hitting nearly $20,000 a penny. It was the most significant financial investment ever. Since then, Bitcoin's value compared to the dollar has decreased, but crypto bulls believe it can improve its performance and take over the rest of the crypto market.

More than ever, investors—both individuals and institutions—have a kind of crypto. This includes very public skeptics such as Jamie Demon, JPMorgan Chase's Chief Executive Officer. The Chicago Mercantile Exchange (CME) provides Bitcoin's Futures options, giving the mainstream sustainability it had not had until its 2017 start. The crypto market is marked by robust potential investment in growth: increased visibility and sense, a relatively low market cap compared with the conventional asset classes, and a steady increase in utility.

Financial Stability

Most US investors consider crypto as an investment risky. The U.S. dollar can be the reserve currency globally and is also one of the planet's most reliable currencies. Crypto is potentially a more stable source of money for a nation such as Venezuela. This is more than just a fantasy or experiment—all of them have doubled their Bitcoin use year after year, Nigeria, Australia, Spain, and Canada.

The public uses Bitcoin to save their lives in countries like Venezuela. The government cannot regulate Bitcoin just as much as it can control a fiat currency. Russia is finding its cryptography and criminalizing all such non-sanctioned rivals. Zimbabweans tend to cryptograph the government's gold-backed money.

Smart Contracts

Imagine that a prosecutor never needs to pay another lawyer. Dream of an immobilization contract without any escrow costs. This is a future where Ethereal advocates believe is real. The intelligent agreement built on the ethereal framework and quantified by the Cryptocurrency of Ether takes the unchangeable, fraud-less blockchain into the law sector. Smart contracts create a 100% safe route for a transaction to be reached without the judiciaries.

Ethereal was too well-received to surpass Bitcoin in terms of new users during the last year. The principle of smart contracts. Developers from ethereal say that ethereal is soon to beat Bitcoin in the number of developers, day-to-day exchanges, and purchases.

Decentralized Social Media

Recent tensions were raised between Facebook and Twitter due to their readiness to regulate their website. They fail according to who you ask. A shared social network is one of the intentional applications of cryptocurrencies. There is no overarching authority in this system to censor divisive content or not to censor it.

The debate over privacy also comes to an end with decentralized social media as no central body is present to collect and sell private data. Invasive ads as the network finance process were replaced by cryptocurrency micropayments. Spam is still unwelcome but is moderated by a smart contract rather than an arbitrary mod.

Disadvantages

The risks of exchange are primarily related to the uncertainty of cryptocurrencies. It is high-risk and speculative, and before you begin trading, you need to understand the risks.

The fluctuations in consumer emotions will lead to sharp price swings. They are unpredictable. There are rarely hundreds, if not thousands of dollars, for the valuation of cryptocurrencies.

It is not regulated. Both governments and central banks currently do not regulate cryptocurrencies. Recently, however, they began to draw further attention. There are concerns such as whether they can be listed as an asset or virtual currency.

They are vulnerable to failures and malware. Technological crashes, human error, or hacking are not entirely avoided.

They can be impacted by forks or disruption. Crypto-monetary trading brings additional risks, such as rough forks or interruption. Before trading these goods, you should become acquainted with these risks. When a complex bifurcation happens, significant price instability may occur all over the case, and we can suspend trade if the underlying market does not deliver stable rates.

Before you start investing, you can ensure you thoroughly understand the risks involved only if you are a professional trader with advanced stock market experience. Trading in cryptocurrencies may not be ideal for everyone.

Cryptocurrency Parameters to Analyze in Investing

Value and Price Are Not Synonyms

If you google "Bitcoin price" you'll see its current value expressed in any currency you choose. This information is useful if you want to know how much capital you need to make an immediate purchase. Apart from that, present price data is essentially useless. In order to be genuinely useful, you need to know the potential value in the context of previous and future (or potential future) prices.

The price of Bitcoin was at one point $0.10, which means an increase to $10,000. Either seems like an extremely high price to pay for the same thing or, if you happen to own some, a phenomenal return on your investment. However, if you know that the price was $20,000 in 2017, $10,000 looks like an intimidating loss. Out of context, a price is just a number that doesn't tell you anything useful.

If you examine a bitcoin chart carefully, you will see that the price has (if you negate short-term volatility) always increased over the long term. This is true of all the major cryptocurrencies including ether and XRP. It is even clearer if you examine the price action on a logarithmic chart, rather than a linear chart.

These charts enable you to see the long-term increase in the price of an asset such as bitcoin, as the number of users rises over time. You can use this to your advantage and buy when the price is contextually low against the backdrop of this constant price increase.

As more people start using bitcoin, the volatility will also increase so that each "wave" of the chart will be larger than the previous one. This is illustrated in the chart below. The boxes represent almost identical price action, but the proportions are larger reflecting the growth of the market. This means that we can expect the next increase in price to also be proportionally larger.

This data suggests that, so long as you take the long-term view, purchasing bitcoin at any price below $20,000 is justified for as long as the adoption trend continues (i.e., Bitcoin continues to be a technology that people want to use).

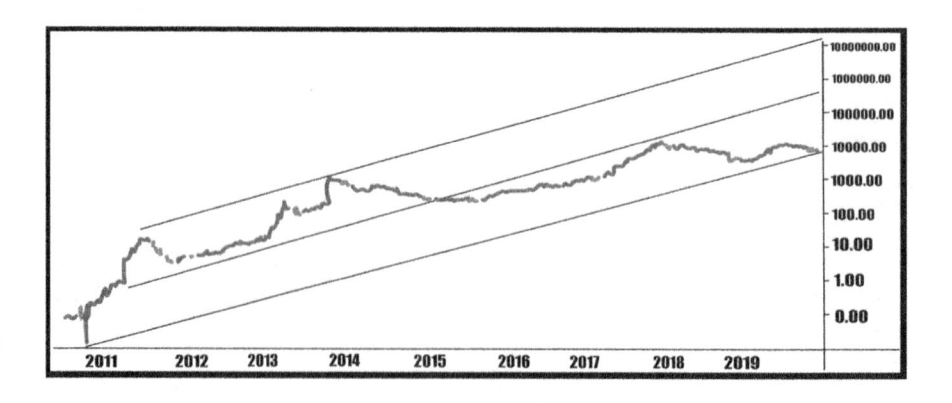

A logarithmic BTC chart all time.

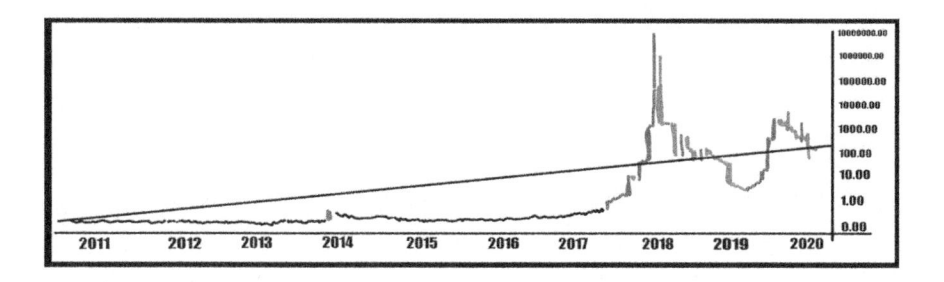

A linear BTC chart all time.

If investors knew with certainty that the price of Bitcoin was going to increase to $500,000 over a specified period, things would be very different. None of them would question a purchase price below $20,000 (or even $400,000) because they would be certain of making a very healthy return. Every investor would be extremely eager to enter the market with all their investment capital. While it's true that nothing in life is certain, we can use data, previous price actions, and statistics to help us determine the most probable outcome.

When valuing new companies with little or no trading history (and, therefore, no agreed price), investors derive a valuation from what are called "fundamentals." We can define these as "usually intangible qualities likely to result in the value of the company increasing or decreasing over a specified time."

OSCAR BUFF

Fundamentals include factors such as the caliber of the directors or senior management team, historical sales figures, and staff retention rates. If any of these are of concern (for example, if staff keep leaving because of toxic management) investors tend to avoid investing in the long-term growth of the company or may even bet against it. Thousands of analysts around the world, who pride themselves on their ability to value companies, are working with fewer data than cryptocurrencies can provide to the diligent investor. The investor just has to know where to look and what to look for.

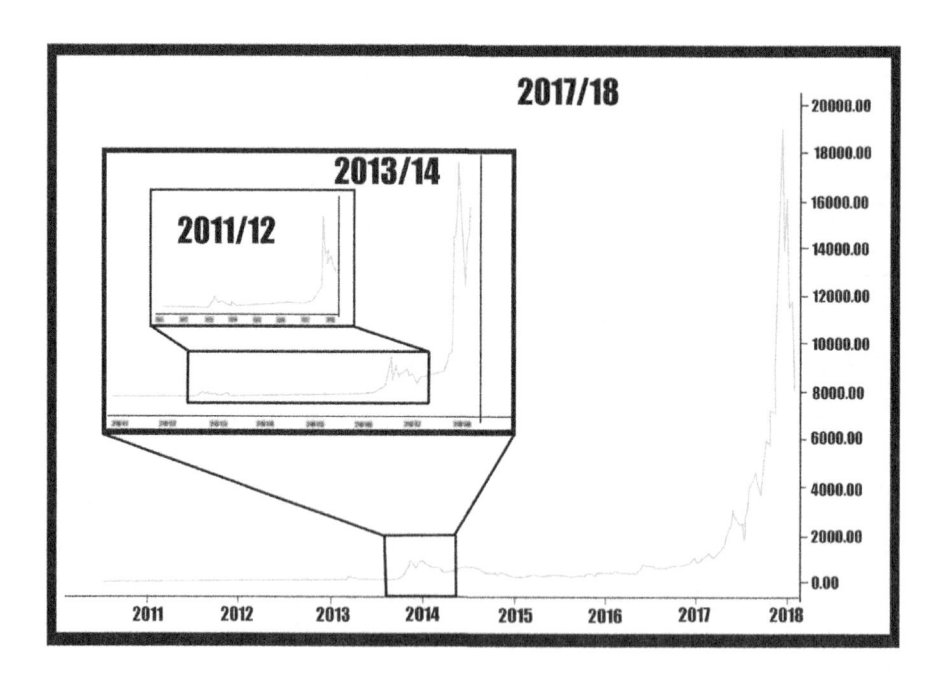

Same price action, proportionally larger waves.

Value investors don't tend to follow the latest fad in technology, fashion, or entertainment. Instead, they invest in companies with strong fundamentals whose brands permeate the fabric of society, such as Apple, Coca-Cola, and Microsoft. Value investors attempt to purchase their shares when the fundamentals are opposed to the price of the share or the dividend yield the company is offering. By holding the stock over decades, they plan on both the share price and the dividend yield to increase over the long-term, when the market increases the price so it is in line with the fundamentals (value). When the discrepancy between the share price and the value of the fundamentals becomes smaller, they may sell in order to invest in a new company with a larger discrepancy.

This is investing (which focuses on long-term potential and profits, over a timeframe measured in years) rather than trading, which takes a short-term perspective (hours to days). An investor only sells when they feel their investment has reached maturity and parity with the long-term fundamentals, rather than reacting to short-term price action caused by volatility.

Examples of strong fundamentals for a company such as Google would be the number of daily searches and whether this is growing or dropping. A strong fundamental of Virgin is a dynamic, ambitious CEO with a track record of success. Many fundamentals are subjective, but they can nonetheless help you to make good decisions, especially when a lot of information is not available or missing.

Investing in strong fundamentally supported cryptocurrencies is less risky than investing in new technology companies. Not only can you use fundamentals to great effect, but you also have historic price data to work from. By looking at the historical data, you can discover what a cryptocurrency was worth at any point in the past and use this to arrive at an informed decision. You never have all the data you'd like to have and it's never 100% reliable. Nonetheless, putting all the available data together can give you a better idea of your risk, expected return, and potential loss.

Countless fundamentals could be relevant to the value of any given cryptocurrency and, therefore, affect your investment decisions. Here are the most important ones you need to know about and consider when planning your investments:

Market Capitalization

This is the total amount of capital invested in the cryptocurrency at any given time and is usually, though not necessarily always, measured in US dollars. The higher the market capitalization, the stronger the cryptocurrency. However, there is a trade-off regarding the potential for extremely profitable returns. The stronger the cryptocurrency market capitalization, the more limited its upward potential tends to be.

Market Share

This is the percentage of the total cryptocurrency market devoted to the cryptocurrency. It indicates how much of the marketplace is adopting or using a particular cryptocurrency. In other words, it gives you a good indication of how many people find cryptocurrency useful. The higher the percentage, the stronger the cryptocurrency. By way of example, Bitcoin is usually above 42%. Small projects with less than 1% of the market can still be worth investing in, but they carry a greater risk of long-term failure and loss of capital.

Transaction Volume

This refers to the number of transactions occurring within a given period. In general terms, the higher the number of transactions, the more viability the cryptocurrency is said to have. Low transaction volume doesn't necessarily mean a cryptocurrency is worthless. It may just not yet be widely adopted (though this could change). On strong trading days, this metric can be deceptive. Traders can initiate transactions worth millions of dollars without using the cryptocurrency for its intended purpose, so this fundamental is only useful when viewed in combination with other strong fundamental reasons to invest.

Development Team and Update Cycle

If the cryptocurrency has a specific development team, who is the leader, and what credentials do they have that would help to develop and strengthen the cryptocurrency? How many people are on the development team? It can be a bit of a challenge to get good information about this fundamental for cryptocurrencies that, like bitcoin, have no employed developers but rely on thousands of volunteers instead.

Generally, the more experienced and suitably qualified the development team behind a cryptocurrency project, the more potential it has as a viable investment opportunity. You can also check how frequently a cryptocurrency project is developed and monitor its progress via a website such as GitHub. Projects that have not had an update for a while (months) may indicate that the project is performing poorly and are to be avoided as viable investment opportunities.

Partnerships with Financial Institutions

Does the cryptocurrency have partnerships in place with pre-existing non-crypto financial institutions? Furthermore, are these institutions supporting or using the cryptocurrency for its intended purpose and deriving a direct benefit? If the answer is yes in both cases, this is a very favorable fundamental. The greater the number and quality of these partnerships (for example, with a major technology company or financial institution) the more likely it is that the cryptocurrency will still exist in 10 years and be trading at a substantially higher price than it is today.

Extent of Adoption

Are people using cryptocurrency to solve the problems it was intended to solve? Is it starting to fulfill its purpose rather than just being hoarded by speculators keen to sell out as soon as the price increases? Bitcoin is being used in genuine transactions every day; some other cryptocurrencies are not. If a cryptocurrency is unlikely to grow in terms of real-world adoption and traction, then it would most likely be replaced by another cryptocurrency that performs a similar (or superior) function and has a larger number of real-world users.

Number of Users

How many people are holding or using the coins? The more users a cryptocurrency has, the higher that cryptocurrency's investment potential. It's also worth asking if the cryptocurrency project has major support from "HODL" investors.

A note of explanation: "HODL" is a misspelling of "hold" which appeared on the Reddit website in the early days of cryptocurrency investing. It has since come to mean "Hold on for Dear Life" and refers to investors who will never sell their coins except to make extremely high returns. In theory, these investors would not only keep their investment if Bitcoin returned to $1, but would buy substantially more. This practice contributes to a steady increase in the price of major cryptocurrencies over time as more and more people "HODL" a particular digital currency.

This list of fundamental properties is by no means exhaustive. There are many more that an investor could consider before deciding whether to purchase any given cryptocurrency. Not all cryptocurrencies have the same fundamental properties and any fundamental strength, which is always at least partly subjective; is constantly fluctuating. The key point is that the greater the number of strong fundamental properties a cryptocurrency has, the more likely an increase in the price and the less risk that you will lose your capital.

It is also worth mentioning that these fundamentals are variables—they can change during a cryptocurrency's life. Assessing fundamentals is one way to evaluate whether a currency represents a good potential investment. However, some cryptocurrencies are all "smoke and mirrors" and never a good investment. You'll need to know how to avoid them.

Avoiding Scamcoins

As with any new technology or investment opportunity, scams are unfortunately part of the cryptocurrency story. Investors have lost billions of dollars by believing scammers and not being sufficiently diligent with their investment decisions. However, before you invest in any crypto project, you can perform some very simple checks that will increase your chances of avoiding scam artists.

Is It Available on Major Exchanges?

While is it true that not all high-quality cryptocurrencies are available on all exchanges, major exchanges such as Coinbase or Binance are unlikely to list a project that is a scam. Naturally, the exchange has an interest in protecting its reputation and conducts thorough due diligence prior to listing a new cryptocurrency. If your potential cryptocurrency investment isn't listed on any major exchange and has existed for a significant amount of time (let's say at least 6 months), then you should avoid investing until you know more about it. At the very least, you will want to know why it isn't listed. (You can find a list of reputable exchanges by clicking the "Exchanges" tab on the website.)

Is There a White Paper?

Every major cryptocurrency has what is called a "white paper." This is a document stating the cryptocurrency's purpose, who developed it, and how. White papers are usually available on the cryptocurrency's website. For a good example of how a white paper is written and presented, look at the Bitcoin white paper published in 2008 (see the "Whitepaper" tab on the website).

Some sophisticated scams may include a (fake) white paper, but they are usually of poor quality with significant omissions and inconsistencies. The presence of a white paper is not a guarantee that the cryptocurrency is a good investment, or even that it isn't a scam. However, if the white paper is of high quality, verifiably authored by credible individuals, and looks legitimate, this generally indicates that the cryptocurrency is a genuine offering and, alongside strong fundamentals, may have investment potential.

How Did You Hear About the Cryptocurrency?

If you hear about a new cryptocurrency via word-of-mouth or an advert, be very cautious. Some cryptocurrency scams apply multi-level marketing techniques in which a "friend" (who may legitimately believe in the project) recommends the currency because they stand to gain something if you go ahead and invest. In effect, they are being bribed to give a positive recommendation and to get you to invest your capital by the scammers.

It's often said that if something sounds too good to be true, it probably is. This doesn't always apply to cryptos because some people have achieved phenomenal returns that seemed "too good to be true" at the time. It is more useful to look for inconsistencies in the business model or rationale of the cryptocurrency. For example, one of the largest scams offered its participants 15% returns per month for life. While achieving 15% profit in a month is certainly possible with cryptocurrency investing, yielding this kind of profit for life is not.

Profit Points

- Assessing the investment potential of cryptocurrencies is challenging but made easier by examining the fundamentals.

- The greater the number of strong fundamental properties a cryptocurrency has, the more likely it is to increase in price, and the less risk there is that you will lose your capital.

- You can avoid most scams via research and critical thinking. Is there a white paper? Does the cryptocurrency appear to solve a real problem (ideally, one that you can witness)? If the investment return sounds implausible look for more evidence. With any cryptocurrency investment, it is always best, when conducting due diligence, to triple-check and check again.

- Use the free crypto-proof valuation tool to find current data on cryptocurrencies and help you assess any coin's investment potential. (It's available under the "Tools" tab on the website).

CHAPTER 9

CRYPTOCURRENCY MINING

When the word "gold mining" was first established, it was intended to refer primarily to the activity of the gold mine, which was the case at the time of its introduction. Despite the fact that it has gained international acceptance, the word has gained in popularity in recent years and is now frequently used to refer to this practice all over the world, particularly in the United States. Cryptocurrency mining or Bitcoin mining is the process through which new cryptocurrencies or Bitcoins are generated and distributed in the cryptocurrency and Bitcoin mining industries, and it is referred to as such in certain areas. Mineral prospectors, also known as miners, are those who own or operate mining equipment in order to search for and gather valuable minerals in their local region. They are also known as gold miners. Bitcoin (or another cryptocurrency) transactions are frequently referred to as "mines," and the processing equipment that is required to discover Bitcoin (or another cryptocurrency) across a distributed network of computers that is then used to complete the transaction is referred to as "mining equipment." After the hashing method has been used to evaluate the data that is included inside the digital signature, it will be used in order to produce the signature itself. This is owing to the fact that the mining process itself is too responsible for this.

In the realm of digital signatures, the phrase "digital signature algorithm" refers to the process that is used to produce digital signatures and is defined as "the mechanism by which digital signatures are generated." As a result, the following has been established: The term "block" refers to a collection of data on the Bitcoin network, which comprises information on transactions that have occurred on the network since the previous block was established. A database of information about transactions that have occurred on the network has been built up since the last block was produced. In the Bitcoin community, it is usual practice to refer to a block on the Bitcoin network as a transaction history; however, this is not necessarily the case in this context; for more details, read the section on transaction histories further down this page. To express gratitude for their efforts, each network member who successfully decrypts the digital signature technique utilized by the network will be awarded bitcoins as a reward. The reward for successfully filtering through massive volumes of "dead rock," which is comprised of hashes that are deemed unsuitable for inclusion in a block of transactions, is a "gold bar," which is in the form of a transaction that generates valuable metals and is received by each miner in the form of a "gold bar." The digital signature of each new block is formed by combining the digital signatures of all of the blocks that have come before it.

When blocks are joined together, a chain of blocks is created, which is referred to as the blockchain network. Each block in the Blockchain network is linked to the next block in the network by a network of connections that connects them all. Each block in the Blockchain network is connected to the next block in the network by a network of links that connects them all. It is estimated that the Blockchain network has thousands of blocks in total. Unlike what the general public believes, the mining business does not provide a source of income that can be obtained by simply plugging in a piece of equipment and waiting for it to begin generating revenue for the equipment's owner. Even though it seems to be so, mining is a difficult and time-consuming activity that, despite its looks, is recognized and compensated economically by the system. The fact that both the Bitcoin client code and the Bitcoin protocol code are available as open-source means that a considerable number of alternative currencies will need to be built, which will take time and will need significant financial investment. Because an excessive number of bitcoins is already in circulation, it is necessary to limit the number of new bitcoins created to the barest minimum, as determined by the technology's developer at the time of its development.

It is necessary to spend significant financial resources in order to generate new coins on a continuous basis. A significant expenditure of financial resources on the side of the government is required to achieve this. These resources include equipment, facilities, cooling systems, power, and other resources, among other things. As a result of this classification, Bitcoin is referred to as "digital gold," and it is represented on the Bitcoin blockchain in the form of gold coins rather than other cryptocurrencies, as a result of this classification. A brief introduction to cryptocurrency mining is provided in this part in order to assist you in better understanding the cryptocurrency mining process and its ramifications.

When it comes to mining, which is referred to as cryptocurrency mining in the cryptocurrency industry, a comprehensive list of every transaction data is compiled and then used to generate a new data block. A Bitcoin transaction will be recorded on the blockchain after it has been completed, and it will be impossible to spend the same amount of Bitcoin more than once at that point. It is anticipated that this would remove the possibility of double-spending entirely (and has been properly confirmed). A means of accomplishing this goal has previously been offered, and it was stated that incorporating transaction data into a permanent and publicly available ledger system would be one approach to doing it. It is no longer possible to add or edit the information contained inside a block after it has been properly integrated. Once a sufficient number of messages have been added to a block that has not yet been verified, the information about the block is updated with the new information that has been discovered. Additionally, the header data contains extra information, a hash from the previous block, and a new hash for the current block (which is the header data). The examples above represent many types of information that may be uncovered.

To ascertain whether or not the unconfirmed block is real, other miners will need to verify your node's integrity. This will indicate whether or not you were successful in completing the assignment successfully. As soon as you have completed the project to their complete satisfaction, they will confirm that you have done so. First and foremost, you must complete the proof-of-work (PoW) procedure and then update the blockchain before you can celebrate the verification of a new block of data that has been added to the blockchain. When a new block of data is verified, it should be celebrated as soon as the blockchain has been updated to reflect the new information. Despite the fact that it demands a large time and effort commitment, this is a very effective method of proclaiming that you have successfully solved a hash and that the other miners can verify your claim. As a result, since it is the most recent block to be added to the blockchain network, it will be put at the end of the network, signaling that the blockchain network as a whole has come to an end. It is necessary to remember that when new blocks are brought into the blockchain network, they are added to the network in the order in which they were created, as mandated by the protocol that is used to produce new blocks in the blockchain network. Before any transaction data can be recorded into the ledger, it must first be encrypted and then decrypted again. This is achieved via the use of public-key cryptography, which is a kind of encryption that anybody may use. If required, both asymmetric encryption methods and symmetric encryption techniques may be used to achieve this goal at the same time if both are available. The hash of each block must be verified by all of the miner nodes that are participating in the blockchain that it is a part of in order for it to be included in the previous chain of blocks that have been previously constructed in order for it to be included in the blockchain that it is a part of.

It may be used to prevent illegal activity as well as to modify already-existing materials, among other things. It is the machines that are utilized throughout the mining process which are responsible for maintaining a record of all transactions, rather than a central authority. According to one research, a new block of data is added to the blockchain with the help of bitcoin mining on an approximately every 10-minute basis, demonstrating that this happens on a nearly daily basis in real-world usage of the cryptocurrency in question. Furthermore, it is safer since it is open to the whole public, which is made possible by the fact that anybody may inspect and update the data held inside it. This makes it more secure. Using your computer to solve the cryptographic hash created by your mining algorithm in order to mine for cryptocurrencies on the Internet is necessary.

If you discover yourself in this situation, you must stay alert until one of the perpetrators is apprehended and brought to justice. If you are successful in completing the task and receiving your reward, you must repeat the procedure until you have reached your goal of correctly solving the riddle and earning a gift, which may take many attempts to accomplish. Finally, a series of fruitless attempts would almost probably end in the great majority of persons quitting the mining process and seeking other sources of revenue to complement their income. First and foremost, you may wonder why someone would go gold mining in the first place. Who knows what type of motive may be at the root of this circumstance? The likelihood of being successful in locating and obtaining a reward is entirely based on chance and luck. If the chances of earning recompense are totally dependent on chance, one must ask why someone would waste their precious time, effort, and money (which might be better spent on the purchase and upkeep of necessary equipment) wasting their valuable time, effort, and money? Because the vast majority of you are almost certainly uninformed of the various cryptocurrency opportunities available to you.

Cryptocurrency names like Bitcoin, Ethereum, and Dash are likely familiar to those of you who are more knowledgeable about the cryptocurrency sector than the rest of us. These are just a few examples. The fact that, in addition to Bitcoin and other cryptocurrencies currently in circulation, there are thousands of more cryptocurrencies available for purchase and exchange. More than 13,400 different cryptocurrencies will be in circulation throughout the world by the time this book is released, representing a considerable rise over the previous year. Given the decentralized nature of cryptocurrencies, their value varies on a frequent basis, and their functioning is defined by an unusually high level of volatility in value throughout the course of the day. Many individuals are being attracted to the convenience of online transactions that are made using digital money rather than conventional currency as time progresses, due to the lower cost and increased convenience that digital money brings. It is because of their ease of use and comfort in transportation that they have gained widespread acceptance.

People who work in the financial industry are becoming more alarmed as the public worry about the present financial institutions growing in popularity among the general population. Having total control over one's financial assets while also preserving one's personal information and identity is something that the vast majority of people want and anticipate having in the near future. The federal government does not have the legal power to know what you purchase or how much money you spend on your fundamental wants and requirements, according to a large number of individuals. They also do not believe that the federal government has the legal ability to know how much money you earn. Some people choose to store their money in their basements or in an old dusty mattress in their attic, believing that this would be more effective than being tracked down by a centralized monetary authority, which they feel will be more successful in the long run. According to the country's constitution, the establishment of centralized financial institutions is forbidden. This practice, therefore, is outlawed in the United States (just kidding). It is possible that when it comes to spending money, individuals would choose to do it in a discrete manner in order to avoid involving the old-style centralized financial authority in the decision-making process. This method has shown to be useful in a number of different situations. Several strategies are available to accomplish this aim, including the use of cryptocurrencies and cryptocurrency mining. Keep in mind that, since the majority of cryptocurrencies are designed to be anonymous (not all and not always, see *Wallet and Exchanges*), people who want to use their assets may do so in the most discreet manner possible by using a cryptocurrency wallet.

Following this advancement, public-key encryption and hash functions are now used in conjunction with one another in order to carry out the crypto-mining process. Thank you very much for all of your hard work. The bitcoin miners are compensated with a tiny percentage of the coins they have mined in exchange for their efforts, and they are rewarded in bitcoins. The importance of remembering that the great majority of persons will not experience a return on their initial investment in the resources they employed should not be overlooked while assessing the strategy. In the event that a cryptocurrency is in great demand (such as Bitcoin), the mining industry will benefit from the incentives offered by the cryptocurrency, even if the cryptocurrency in question is relatively uncommon. Coins such as bitcoin and ether are acquiring broad acceptability throughout the globe at an alarming pace, despite the fact that they were only invented a few years ago. This is surprising given the fact that they are still in their infancy. As a consequence of the growth in the number of people who do business with them, store their products for later use, and eat their goods in recent years, they have witnessed a considerable increase in the number of people who do business with them, store their items for later use, and consume their goods.

For example, if you want to know everything about a mining company, all you have to do is search for its name, as seen in the example below. CPUs are employed in the Bitcoin mining process, although they are a less-than-efficient technique of allocating time and resources when compared to other methods. Simple? Yes! I can say clearly and without hesitation in response to your question. Effective? We believe that this is not the case in this particular circumstance. Because CPU mining is more time-consuming and inefficient than other mining techniques, consumers who choose CPU mining instead of other mining methods may have to wait for a long period of time before seeing any possible returns on their investments. Consumption expenditures, such as those linked with energy and cooling operations, are quite infrequent in the real world. It seems unlikely that the great majority of consumers will be able to recuperate their expenditures if the prices of energy and cooling processes are returned to them.

Generally speaking, this strategy is advantageous if your power usage is moderate and your CPUs are kept at an acceptable level of cooling during the workday, which is the situation in the vast majority of cases nowadays. After all, what rationale could there possibly be for continuing to pursue a mining approach that would be unprofitable on every level? This is because everyone who has access to a computer, particularly a desktop computer, can start this kind of mining. It makes no difference how many laptop computers are used to carry out the mining operation; due to the extreme heat generated, all of the circuits in each laptop will fail within a few hours of the activity being initiated. If you are interested in cryptocurrency mining and have a strong desire to do so but do not have a thorough grasp of the issue, you may find that doing so is financially advantageous. Individuals who mine for a few days before realizing that they would not be able to gain any money from their efforts are feasible, though.

When most people hear the term "cryptocurrency mining," the first thing that comes to mind is "graphics processing unit mining." GPU mining rigs are the most expensive mining rigs presently available on the market, and they are also the most complex.

Therefore, a GPU mining setup made from the disassembled components would cost some thousand dollars, but the user would see money in their account much more rapidly than they would with typical CPU mining. A GPU design is often made up of the following components: the CPU, motherboard, cooling system, frame, and graphics cards, to mention a few. A GPU design uses a variety of other components that may be utilized either in addition to or in place of the ones mentioned above. In recent years, there has been a significant increase in the usage of graphics cards for bitcoin mining.

As far as mining is concerned, in order to achieve good performance, it is very important the location where the mining is done, the main characteristics being the cost of the energy used, the meteorological temperature, which, if it is cold, saves cooling costs, and, the host state, which must be neutral or friendly to this kind of activity.

CHAPTER 10

BITCOIN WALLETS, STORAGE, AND TRANSACTIONS

Before you can actually get or spend Bitcoins, you need to have a place to put them. Bitcoins are stored in a digital Bitcoin address, which is called a wallet. There are several different types of Bitcoin wallets, and we'll look at some of the most popular ones and go over how to create your own. Before we get into how to choose and create your wallet, let's look a bit more closely at how Bitcoin wallets work.

The crypto in the term "cryptocurrency" is a reference to cryptography, which is the study of secure communication. Contemporary cryptography relies heavily on complex mathematical algorithms that are deciphered by computers. To send messages containing sensitive information, people often encrypt their emails so that only the intended recipient will be able to decipher them. To a third party, encrypted emails will usually appear as complete nonsense, and unless they have the special password or key to decrypt the message, they will not be able to decipher the contents.

While modern encryption is almost always associated with digital information, cryptography has been around for centuries. Used predominantly by militaries, earlier forms of encryption included things like using secret codes to send messages through hostile territory. One example of Classical cryptography is the "Caesar Cypher," allegedly invented by Julius Caesar to communicate with his generals. The Caesar Cypher is a simple substitution cypher where certain letters in the original message are substituted with letters a specific number down from the original, creating a sort of "word scramble" that could only be understood if you knew the number of the shift and could then reverse the process to decipher the message.

Today, of course, encryption is typically a much more complex mathematical process. We all use different forms of encryption regularly, whether we are conscious of it or not, such as an ATM pin number to access your bank account or the simple practice of using a password to unlock your phone. For sending sensitive information, many people use more complex systems with multiple layers of heavy-duty encryption.

Bitcoin wallets are secured using a kind of asymmetric encryption, sometimes also called "public-key cryptography." If you have used tools like PGP encryption for sending email, this might sound familiar. If not, don't worry! Once again some wild math stuff happens in the background, but actually using most wallets is very straightforward.

There are two important parts to all standard Bitcoin wallets: a public key and a private key. These two keys are generated by an algorithm and usually just look like long strings of random letters and numbers.

The Public Key

The public key is the address for your Bitcoin wallet. This is a unique digital address, sort of like your "email address for Bitcoin." Everybody can see your public key. People will use this address, your public key, to send Bitcoin to you. Your public key address will also be recorded on the blockchain when you make a transaction, as Bitcoins either move into your wallet from somewhere else or you send Bitcoins from your wallet to another wallet's address (i.e., someone else's public key). Depending on how your Bitcoin wallet is set up, your public key may be linked to your identity, either directly or indirectly. In fact, unless you are very intentional about taking advanced security measures to ensure your privacy, you should assume that someone can link your public key address to your identity.

The Private Key

If your public key is like your "email address" for Bitcoin, the private key is like your password. Your private key is for your eyes only, and this is what allows you to access the contents of your wallet and send Bitcoins to other people.

When you send Bitcoin to someone else, it is the combination of

OSCAR BUFF

their public key and your private key that makes the transaction valid. Your private key tells the system "Hey, I am really the owner of this wallet," and the public key tells it "this other wallet is where the Bitcoins should go."

Your private key is extremely important! If anyone else gets access to your private key, such as a hacker, they will be able to control your funds. There is pretty much no recourse if this happens, which is why it is vital to keep your private key secure. Unlike an email password, you can't simply "reset" your private key if you misplace it, so be careful. If you lose your private key, there is essentially no way to recover it and you will not be able to access your bitcoins!

Just as there are many different email providers available, there are also many options for creating a Bitcoin wallet. We will look at some of the most popular ways to create a wallet for Bitcoin, with the pros and cons of each.

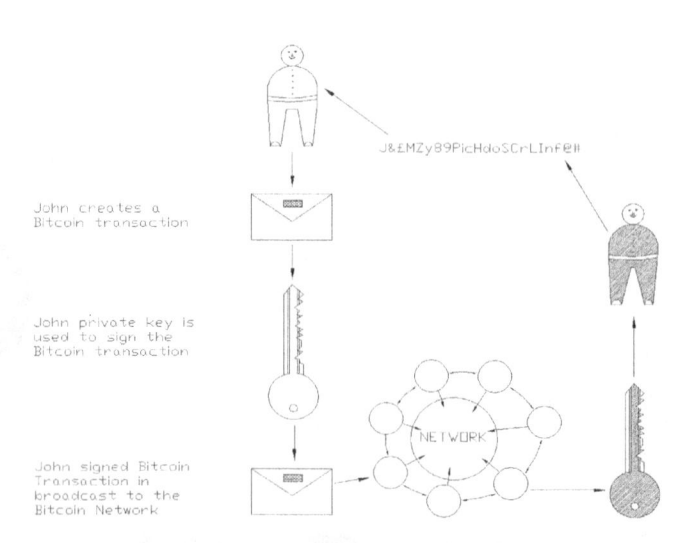

John creates a Bitcoin transaction

John private key is used to sign the Bitcoin transaction

John signed Bitcoin Transaction in broadcast to the Bitcoin Network

J&£MZy89PicHdoSCrLInF@ll

NETWORK

Carl generates a new Bitcoin address and tells it to John. He keeps the associated private key secret

Carl can verify with the network that transaction has been place. Only Carl can spend Bitcoin from this address as he is the only one in possession of the private key

114

Creating a Bitcoin Wallet

Before we dive into some of the different types of Bitcoin wallets, it is important to note that Bitcoin transactions are irreversible! If you are just getting started with Bitcoin, you will want to be sure to have a solid understanding of how your wallet works before making any major transactions.

Some wallets are more complex but offer greater levels of security and anonymity. Others are a bit easier but come with more reliance on a third party, such as a Bitcoin exchange. There are many different opinions throughout the Bitcoin community concerning best practices when it comes to wallets, and this space changes frequently as new options enter the market. Some people create a new wallet address for every single transaction and keep their Bitcoins spread out across multiple wallets. Some people keep all of their Bitcoins in one wallet and use that forever, some others use one wallet for fast and small payments like a coffee or a book—of course, where they're accepted—and another to store more value. One of these easy-to-use wallets is BlueWallet which uses a lightning network to make faster movements.

You can visit https://bitcoin.org/en/choose-your-wallet to see some of the many options available for creating a wallet, including mobile, desktop, hardware, and online wallets. Whatever form of wallet you end up using, it is important to remember that Bitcoin is real money and can be lost or stolen. We will cover the basics here, but if you plan to deal with large sums it is good to become familiar with some more advanced security measures to protect your digital assets.

Online Wallets

Online wallets are one of the most abundant forms of Bitcoin wallet. Several online services, such as Bitcoin exchanges, offer the ability to store your funds online through one of their wallets. These wallets are easy to create, but generally, anything that keeps your assets online is considered to be less secure. In fact, several of these services have been hacked or suffered from major security breaches in the past.

Obviously, anything that is connected to the Internet is more vulnerable to hacking or malware than something that is not on the Internet. Bitcoin wallets are no exception. Many people choose to keep the bulk of their Bitcoin offline and also maintain an online wallet with a small number of funds for quick and easy online transactions.

Desktop/Mobile Wallets

There are a few options out there to create Bitcoin wallets that can be stored on your computer and/or mobile phone. To an extent, these can offer more security than online storage through a third-party service. Once again, however, any device that is connected to the Internet is potentially vulnerable to malware. Unless you have a computer that you never connect to the Internet (this is called "air-gapped,") you can still be susceptible to cyber-attacks.

Many wallets come with additional layers of encryption, password protection, and other security features built-in, which can drastically reduce the risks. You will also have the option to create backups and add additional layers of encryption, which is a good idea. Generally, however, if you are dealing with a significant amount of Bitcoin, the safest way to store them is offline.

Cold Storage

Keeping your Bitcoin wallet offline, in a secure location, is generally considered to be the most secure way to store Bitcoin. It is common practice for people to keep the bulk of their Bitcoin offline, which is commonly called "cold storage," and only keep small amounts online for regular transactions. The downside to creating and using a cold storage wallet is that to do it effectively can be somewhat technically advanced. Services like BitKey, Armory, and others provide assistance in creating secure offline wallets.

Hardware Wallets

Hardware wallets are a popular combination of security and efficiency. As the name implies, these are physical devices, similar in appearance to a USB drive or keychain that are created with the sole purpose of storing Bitcoin. In fact, many hardware wallets use a USB to connect to a computer for making transactions. Even when connected to a compromised computer, good hardware wallets are immune to the kind of malware and viruses that can affect software wallets. Security, ease of use, and recovery options vary between models, so it is wise to spend some time reading reviews and comparing the features of different devices.

Choosing the Best Wallet

We've touched on some of the most popular options, but there are other methods of wallet creation out there. Security, complexity, and other features hold different priority levels for different people. Particularly for those who are planning to make a serious investment in Bitcoin, choosing a secure wallet option is highly recommended, even if it may require some additional legwork to set it up properly. Reading reviews, watching explainer videos, and asking around in Bitcoin forums, such as bitcointalk.org, are good ways to stay informed, ask questions, and choose the best wallet for your needs.

How Do I Get Bitcoin?

Once you have somewhere to put your funds, you can actually get some Bitcoin! There are several ways that someone can get Bitcoin, but the most common are:

- By exchanging fiat currency for Bitcoin through an exchange

- Getting Bitcoin from someone else who already has Bitcoin

- Bitcoin mining

We will look at all of these methods, but before we dive in we should step back and look at a more fundamental question: Where do Bitcoins come from?

Where Do Bitcoins Come From?

Who "makes" bitcoins? This is an important question, and it is related to another issue that you may be wondering about: how is the value of bitcoin determined?

To answer both of these questions, it is helpful to look briefly at where traditional fiat currency comes from. Broadly speaking, governments and institutions control the printing of paper money. The amount of money that is printed impacts the value of that currency in the global financial market. The economics behind how this all works can get pretty complicated, but in a nutshell: the more money the government prints, the less value that currency generally has. In economic terms, this principle is often referred to as "scarcity," meaning that the less there is of something and the more people that want it, the more value that thing has. This concept applies to commodities, fiat currencies, and Bitcoin.

There are many examples throughout history of situations where a government has printed tons of paper money to cover short-term expenses (almost always related to war), and as a result, the value of that currency has plummeted. Perhaps the most renowned example of this is the hyperinflation that occurred in Germany's Weimer Republic after World War I. People famously wallpapered their houses with paper money because it had so little value.

One significant way that Bitcoin is different than fiat currency is that there is a hard cap on the number of Bitcoins that will be created. No more than 21 million Bitcoins will ever exist. The last Bitcoin is estimated to appear sometime around the year 2140. This built-in scarcity is one crucial aspect of how the value of Bitcoin is determined.

Still, however, we have not really answered the question of where Bitcoins actually come from. The short answer is that they are "mined" by Bitcoin miners.

Buying Bitcoin

While there is still opportunity in mining, it is definitely not the most straightforward way to get your hands on some Bitcoin. It is much faster and easier to get existing Bitcoin from somewhere else, rather than trying to mine new Bitcoin.

When it comes to acquiring Bitcoin in this way, you have several options. No matter which route you take, you will need to set up a Bitcoin wallet to receive and store your funds.

Bitcoin Exchanges

In many countries, the easiest way to buy Bitcoin with fiat currency is through an online exchange. Bitcoin exchanges work essentially just like any other currency exchange, where you use one currency to buy another. For example, Coinbase (coinbase.com) is one of the most popular Bitcoin exchanges in the US. Coinbase is an online platform that creates a Bitcoin wallet for you, lets you connect your bank account, and buy or sell Bitcoin through a very simple user interface.

Most Bitcoin exchanges involve transaction fees, and Coinbase is no exception. While it is technically free to use most Bitcoin exchanges, there will be percentage fees associated with most or all transactions. It is also not uncommon to experience delays when transacting through exchanges, which can range from mildly inconvenient to debilitating. Becoming familiar with the process and factoring fees and delay times into your transactions will make things run much more smoothly.

Most exchanges that allow you to buy Bitcoin with fiat currency will require you to link to a bank account and enter some personal information. This allows for fast, convenient movement between fiat currency and Bitcoin. Once again, it will be worth it to do some research and be sure to use an exchange that can demonstrate some longevity and has a good reputation.

Even then, it is generally not a good idea to store all or most of your Bitcoin in an online exchange. Mt. Gox, famously, was the world's dominant Bitcoin exchange for several years. At the height of its popularity, Mt. Gox handled around 70% of the world's total Bitcoin transactions. Then, in 2014, there was a massive security breach and approximately 850,000 bitcoins were lost or stolen under somewhat mysterious circumstances. Exchanges are useful for moving funds between Bitcoin and fiat, trading, and actively transacting with Bitcoin, but the Mt. Gox fiasco is a good example of why it is not the best idea to keep all of your assets stored in an online exchange.

Bitcoin ATMs

Another way to buy Bitcoin that is becoming increasingly popular is through Bitcoin ATMs. These devices are cropping up all over the place, from malls to airports to city centers. They look a lot like traditional ATMs, but there are some important differences. Primarily, Bitcoin ATMs don't connect to any banks. They are connected—through the Internet—only to the universe of the Bitcoin network. Many Bitcoin ATMs allow for bidirectional exchange, meaning that you can either insert cash to be converted to Bitcoin and transferred to a public key address, or you can have Bitcoins from your own account converted into cash and dispensed by the machine. Some only handle transfers one way or the other.

ATMs can provide a more anonymous way to buy into Bitcoin without syncing your bank account to a platform like Coinbase. However, there may be high transaction fees and limits on how much you can deposit or withdraw depending on the machine. One way that you can search for Bitcoin ATMs in your area is by using the Coin ATM Radar website at https://coinatmradar.com/.

Getting Bitcoin from Someone Else

Since the very beginning of Bitcoin, one of the most common ways to get started with the currency has been to find someone willing to gift or sell some to you. As Bitcoin is a digital asset, it should not be too surprising that much of the Bitcoin community exists online. Forums such as bitcointalk.org or Reddit's r/bitcoin are good places to engage with other Bitcoin users. Some Bitcoin enthusiasts are happy to donate a small amount to a newcomer to help them establish their first wallet. After all, the more people that use Bitcoin, the higher the demand, thus, the more valuable it will become, at least in theory. Through that lens, it makes sense from a long-term financial perspective to help new users get started even if means spending a little of your own coin initially.

There are also a variety of tools online to find local Bitcoin exchanges, where people actually meet up offline, in person, to trade with Bitcoin. This can be a great way to avoid transaction fees, meet fellow Bitcoin enthusiasts in your area, and potentially increase the level of transaction anonymity. As with any scenario that involves meeting someone "from the Internet," use your judgment if meeting up to exchange Bitcoin locally.

CHAPTER 11

Cryptocurrency Top Exchanges

Much like you need to use a platform to change money into different currencies, the same can be said for cryptocurrencies. Cryptocurrency exchanges normally facilitate exchanges between different cryptocurrencies as well as fiat currencies. The cryptocurrency exchanges tend to act as the middleman between both the buyer and the seller.

Centralized and Decentralized Exchanges

There are two different types of exchanges, and they have their fair share of differences. The most common and popular form of exchange is the centralized exchange, where the exchange official acts as a third party between the buyer and the seller. It is said that about 99% of all exchanges do occur via these platforms, and as a beginner, it is certainly recommended to start this way as well.

Many advantages come alongside this form of exchange.

For example, the centralized platform is far more user-friendly, offering a familiar as well as a friendly way of trading in comparison to peer-to-peer transactions (decentralized exchanges), which can grow to be quite complex. Simplicity is certainly helpful in any format.

This platform is also far more reliable, adding an extra layer of security when one is actually trading. However, centralized exchanges are at a higher risk of hacking. There were many incidents where hacking has occurred, meaning extra work and effort have to be put in to trust the security of the platform software. Many exchanges hold the value of millions to even potentially billions of dollars worth of money, which makes it a huge digital target.

There are also a lot of transaction fees that come with working on centralized exchanges. The fees will depend on the exchange company you use. You also need to take into account how active you are as a trader because the costs can add up pretty quickly.

On the other hand, decentralized exchanges basically allow users to perform peer-to-peer transactions, where you are performing the exchanges directly with the people themselves rather than through a middleman.

When it comes to this platform, there is an automatically reduced risk of hacking, mainly because no one has the need to share third-party information, and because it does not have much popularity, it is much less likely to be a target. These exchanges are automatically far safer in regard to cybercrime.

Market manipulation is a lot more difficult to build in a decentralized system. This is a massive advantage as it gives users a more even playing field. There is a lot of protection from both wash and fake trading.

One of the biggest advantages of crypto is its anonymous nature, so it is no surprise that having a decentralized exchange would play on the advantage of being anonymous as well. Therefore, you can use this platform with the knowledge that you will remain completely anonymous.

However, as mentioned before, decentralized exchanges are a very complex system, which means more time and effort needs to be spent on figuring the exchanges out. This can be very daunting for a beginner, and should only be used if you prefer the advantages of the decentralized system above the centralized system.

Cryptocurrency Exchanges to Consider

Binance

One of the largest cryptocurrency exchanges, in comparison to the trading volume, is Binance. Binance was published by a man named Changpen Zhao in 2017 in China. It has established a reputation of being one of the most reliable exchanges in the crypto trading world. Due to the hurdles faced in China, Binance is now being operated on the Malta islands in Europe. In September 2019, it also launched a platform specifically dedicated to the United States, called Binance US, which is compliant with the regulatory framework of the United States.

Binance is also one of the few exchanges that do not have fake trading volume or even wash trading activities. This means that it is a very transparent and open company. The more transparency that comes with a business, the better.

Binance has also focused on keeping itself up to date with the latest software and technology, making sure to keep up with the competition that is always rapidly advancing. It has managed to establish itself as one of the most popular gateways in the world of crypto.

Binance's History

Binance has attracted a lot of attention due to the cryptocurrency it trades, such as Ethereum and Bitcoin, as well as smaller tokens that are indeed micro-capped. Each token is needed to first fulfill all the requirements, as listed in the Binance rules before being run on this platform.

In 2019, Binance experienced a hack, where the thieves got away with $40 million in Bitcoin. However, the Binance SAFU

(Secure Asset Fund Users) Fund had compensated for all the losses, and all the traders who suffered losses were reimbursed. This act certainly boosted Binance's popularity in the entirety of the crypto world.

SAFU is the emergency insurance that was implemented in 2018 as a way to protect traders' funds while they are using the exchange. Having your money insured adds a lot of extra security while you are using the exchange platform, which is especially ideal for a beginner.

Binance's Token

Even Binance has its own native token, called the Binance Coin or BNB, which adds a certain element of competition for its trading fee. The trading fee is reduced when using the platform's token.

Opening a Binance Account

First, you will need to open an account by heading over to the Binance webpage, and you can start off by registering your email address and adding a password. Make sure again that the password you choose is long and complex, as you don't want to be hacked. Again, consider opening up two-factor authentication.

You will need to confirm your own personal details, as a

verification of your identity will be required (as expected with a centralized project). This may take a while, as they are very focused on anti-laundering as well as avoiding criminal hubs (which in essence, boosts the security of using the platform, as you would want to make sure you are not dealing with criminals).

Then, after completing the verification process, you can add your funds using either a debit/credit card or bank account, depending on what exactly is supported in your country. Otherwise, you can consider purchasing Bitcoin or Ethereum somewhere else, such as Coinbase, and depositing them onto this platform. When you make the deposit, you can normally start trading within 20 minutes after the deposit has officially been confirmed.

Then you can finally start your journey of trading and investing. You can head to the "Exchange" button that is reflected on the top of the screen, and you can even choose if you want a basic or advanced chart/interface platform to use. This all depends on what you are more comfortable with, assuming you have undergone paper trading and other training before jumping into live training.

eToro

eToro is a cheap and professional exchange used by some of the top traders in the world. It is an accessible trading platform that has cleverly devised a social element into investing. They were first launched in early 2006, and are now one of the world's largest communities in investment, with over 4.5 million users.

eToro has a unique feature called the "copied trader," where a person can sort through the variety of users and check out their trading history. This is especially handy if you are still learning how to trade and would like to see the choices others have made (don't copycat). Rather than having to ask the traders, you are free to view the decisions made and whether they were truly successful or not. If you do find someone whose trading choices seem to be doing well, you have the option to allocate funds that can automatically copy the trade. (This means the choices made with funding are in their hands rather than yours, and as the book pushes against it. So you know it is an option, but rather consider studying and learning from them as you build your own path.)

There is another program on eToro called the "popular investor program." It acts as a reward system for the number of copiers a specific person has (how many people copy your style and strategy of trading). This boosts the incentive to trade wisely, as people will only copy what they deem to be successful.

With the features tagged on eToro, you can consider this to be a great learning platform, and if you want to familiarize yourself with it without too much of a commitment, you can check it out on a demo account.

Again, before signing up, make sure you understand the basics of trading, and start small. It is never recommended to start investing large amounts of money as a beginner.

Opening an eToro Account

First, you will need to sign up at eToro.com; it is not an extensive application and is quite easy to set up. They do require your phone number in order to boost the security of your account.

It is recommended not to trade using CFD (Contract for Difference Trading) products, as most investors suffer a loss when deciding to do this. So keep this in mind as you start trading.

Next, you will want to fully complete your profile. This is when you input your basic personal information—basically verifying who you are and have to answer a couple of trading questions. You don't have to be too concerned about the answers but answer honestly.

Next, you will be directed to the place of deposit, where the minimum amount is normally $200.

Take your time browsing eToro, familiarizing yourself with this platform. You can start by creating a watchlist. This is creating lists of people whose trades you are interested in observing and perhaps considering copying if you want to.

Build your portfolio, which is the center of your journey. Here you can monitor the level of your performance, as well as watch your live trades unfold.

There is also a news feed you can watch, as this is the platform where people keep you updated on what they have been doing recently. This builds a closer community, as many people help each other along with their overall success.

Copy people are the very heart of the community. You can search through many of the traders you want to follow, or if you do so, choose to copy.

Robinhood

This is not the legendary archer from the old tales, but rather, this Robinhood is another exchange platform for you to consider. Robinhood has been trending for quite some time, and many experts agree that it is likely to grow in popularity over time. As a crypto investor, you will be more interested in Robinhood Crypto, which acts as the exchange platform for cryptocurrency reviews.

The Robinhood Crypto app truly brought a new item to market in the mobile world. It made the promises of a far easier trading platform (again, ideal for beginners), and garnered the reputation of making trading life a lot simpler for everyone who decides to use it.

Robinhood Crypto supports many of the top cryptocurrencies, which allows you to trade in comfort and ease, and you can deposit or sell crypto to purchase the coins immediately. However, using other items, such as EFT (Electronic Funds Transfer) or stocks, may take up to 3 days to fulfill a trade.

Naturally, there has been a rise in concern about security itself on the crypto app. However, Robinhood did revert to using both online and offline wallets. As already said, offline wallets are far safer, thus boosting the overall security of using Robinhood.

The majority of all the coins are kept in cold storage, and the company also carries insurance to make up for cybersecurity attacks and potential breaches.

However, Robinhood Crypto does have its fair share of limitations: one is the inability to withdraw your coins and the other is that you cannot transfer the cryptocurrencies elsewhere in your crypto wallet. However, Robinhood Crypto is working on correcting this limitation and upgrading itself to become more user-friendly.

How Robinhood Works

If you have a Robinhood account, it means you have instant access to the Robinhood Crypto account, and even instant access to buying crypto. If you don't, it may take some time to set everything up, including the verification process.

If you have sales from ETFs, it means the money you put in will take a little while longer to arrive, considering you are dealing with the middleman (your bank) and the middleman of the exchange (centralized). This is where patience is needed, but keep in mind you are signing up with Robinhood for its simplicity. If you are struggling to understand the heavy complexities of trading, then perhaps it is best to build your experience on the platform itself.

However, any proceeds that do come from crypto sales are

immediately available for your use. And the moment you have the necessary funds, you can focus on buying the coins and start trading as soon as possible.

Selling the coins is as simplified as buying the coins on this app, and all you need to do is navigate the details page, insert the necessary information, and proceed with the sale itself. The moment the coins are sold, you can move on to your next venture with the funds you have received, making this a very effective and efficient trading platform, without the concern of having to wait days or weeks for money to arrive at your door after a trade.

Robinhood itself has taken measures to protect you from the volatile nature of the market, placing a collar on which you can either buy or sell at certain prices that fits within a specific range.

You also can use a limit order, programming your account to buy or sell crypto once it reaches a certain price. This is ideal for certain strategies and will allow you to stay safe from excessive losses while you are asleep (as you can't trade and stay up to date 24/7 unless you intend to go mad). This is a layer of protection, reducing the amount of loss you may receive when the market does not go in a good direction, but also picks up on opportunities that you may miss while you are away. It is an artificial intelligence that does the work of monitoring the trading activities 24/7 while you deal with other priorities.

Robinhood has gained most of its popularity through the design of the app itself. The app is very simple and easy, along with an appealing/aesthetic interface. It also happens to incorporate some of the latest technology, such as a biometric account where you can use your thumbprint to gain access or even your facial ID.

For the purchasing as well as selling of crypto, Robinhood is very easy and simple to use. Literally, with a couple of taps and swipes and clever strategizing (as a savvy investor should), you could easily complete a trade in a matter of minutes. And you can sell it at a rapid pace as well when need be. This certainly makes crypto more interesting for those who struggle to concentrate or figure out the inner workings of a trade. And again, this is quite ideal for a beginner who is still working on figuring everything out when it comes to cryptocurrency trading.

Robinhood also focuses on lower fees in comparison to the "higher-level" trading sites. To help with people starting out and evening out the playing field, they have removed one of the biggest barriers that come with trading on exchange platforms: the excessively high trading fees.

This means your sales and trades can work with smaller numbers without the trading fees eating up all your profits, so it is easier to start slow on this platform and still make a profit, regardless of the size of your trade (unless you go lower than the trading fee itself, which is not recommended).

However, there are a few drawbacks that come with trading on this app. One of them that had been mentioned before, is its functionality. Withdrawal is normally quite an issue, and although you are able to withdraw to your bank account, this does mean incorporating the traditional capital tax that comes alongside it (making the withdrawal of your crypto quite expensive).

There is also a concerning lack of transparency that comes with these prices. Some "fees" that are supposedly free are just tacked on with the prices people deem the cryptocurrency to be, and this is where Robinhood is actually making the money.

And the team of Robinhood itself has made no comments on the settings of the price of the app, which again, in and of itself can be quite a concerning matter. Transparency is always a big recommendation when it comes to businesses: the less transparency, the more issues the company itself may be trying to hide.

There are also a couple of security concerns, although, unlike some other exchanges, there have been no reports of any large-scale hacks. However, there has been a fair share of cases of isolated hacking occurring in accounts. So the security that is offered on the app is not altogether riskier nor altogether safer than what is being offered on other exchanges. You will have to keep this in mind if safety is a huge priority for you.

So after seeing a little more about Robinhood, you may be

wondering whether it is really the right app for you. Each exchange certainly brings something a little different to the table, and it is up to you to decide which exchange suits you the best.

Other Top Exchanges to Consider

Now, having looked in-depth at some of the top exchanges you can consider as a beginner, here is a peek at some of the other top exchanges you can use:

Coinbase

Coinbase and Coinbase Pro have proven to have simplified and easy forms of transactions. The software itself is very transparent, with strong security latched onto it. It is also a very popular form of exchange, and as you work with cryptocurrency and trading you will most likely hear about Coinbase.

Coinbase has a solid variety of altcoins you can trade with. It is also quite user-friendly, and the level of liquidity tacked onto it is high.

But keep in mind, that the prices are higher if you are not using Coinbase Pro (trading fees), and a person does not have actual control over their wallet keys. This means that you may need to have another wallet outside of the exchange to store the majority of your coins to make sure they are fully secure.

Coinbase also has a lot of issues with fraudulent coins as well as exchanges that have been quite shady. This means many people avoid these exchanges due to security and higher chances of getting caught in a scam. But Coinbase has offered wallets that are insured for investors as well as insurance for any data breaches that may occur. If you are more advanced, you may consider getting Coinbase Pro, which is more complex, but has a far greater variety of options when it comes to both charts and indicators. This is if you want to trade at a higher level, and would like to have the tools to deal with that.

Cash App

Cash App is another user-friendly exchange app you can use that has quite a few flexible options available, such as the use of other crypto wallets and withdrawals. It is a peer-to-peer money transfer that can work like Venmo or even Zelle. You also can withdraw Bitcoin itself if you want, and again, being user-friendly makes the life of a trader a lot easier, as there are many fewer frustrations and issues you would have to face.

However, it only actually supports the use of Bitcoin and not any other crypto. There is also a 3% charge when you are sending money through your credit card, and you have a set number of days as well weekly withdrawal limits.

Cash App allows users to invest in other stocks, Bitcoin, or EFTs in a way that Robinhood can as well. It has a simplified mobile interface, making it ideal for people who are investing for the very first time and for beginners who are very much interested in buying Bitcoin.

Having the ability to withdraw your crypto from an exchange is important in the crypto community. With Robinhood, although you can both invest and trade in your cryptocurrencies, you cannot actually withdraw the crypto and spend it in any way you desire. With the Cash App, you are fully capable of doing so, but you are actually still unable to gain control of your private keys, which is always a security issue, as you may struggle to prove or gain ownership of the coin if you are not careful.

BiSQ

This is by far one of the best-decentralized forms of exchanges out there. BiSQ is open-source software that does not have any KYC (Know Your Customer) requirements and is available if you are interested in dabbling in decentralized exchanges in the near future. There are more than 25 varied options you have to pay for, and you can also use it on a mobile app both for Android and also for iOS.

However, the transaction speeds are known to be quite slow, and considering the lack of popularity in using trading volumes, that can be quite slow as well. It is not exactly designed for active forms of trading either.

Following the premise that Bitcoin has set down, there is

no requirement for you to legally provide any identification, location, or even nationality on BiSQ. For someone who likes to stay anonymous, this is certainly one of the largest benefits. Considering that many people use crypto for the exact same reason, why not use an exchange that has the same goals?

Many argue against the possibility of giving opportunities to criminal activities. There is a flip-side, where people can open accounts that have less-developed banking systems. All you really need is an Internet connection. There are millions of people around the world that have minimal access to a bank, which means at the end of the day it inhibits them from trading if they want to. BiSQ very much provides them this opportunity, as it is a good solution for the most part.

It is a downloadable form of software. There is no central point that can fail or be taken down. There is no main point of authority, which means no one ever has any control over the funds of the user, which is vastly different from centralized exchanges. For example, Coinbase, a centralized exchange has every right to seize the funds you have if they deem your activities to be suspicious, regardless of whether what you are doing is actually legal in your specific location.

BISQ is also instantly accessible to anyone who has access to the Internet and has a computer or a smartphone. This certainly makes it ideal for anyone who wants to have privacy.

A person has to take into account the lower trading volumes

and slower transactions, but for some people, the benefits far outweigh the drawbacks. And again, it is up to you to decide.

When you are looking for a cryptocurrency trading or investing platform, it is best to choose the exchange that suits your goals. Whether it may be cheaper fees, easier design, or even a variety of coins, these are all matters you will have to consider when approaching the exchange. So, it is best to have your goals in place first before deciding on the exchange, rather than adapting to the exchange. After all, this is your journey, and you best make sure you are actually comfortable with the steps you are taking.

CHAPTER 12

How to Buy a Cryptocurrency

Choose a Cryptocurrency Broker or Cryptocurrency Exchange

Before you can obtain cryptocurrencies, you'll need to look for a broker or exchange. Both allow you to develop cryptocurrency, but there are a few vital distinctions to bear in mind.

Cryptocurrency Exchange

To trade cryptocurrencies, buyers and sellers must cooperate on a cryptocurrency exchange. For beginner crypto investors, deals might be scary because of their more complicated interfaces, including several trading kinds and detailed performance charts. Coinbase, Gemini, and Binance are a few well crypto exchanges. Even though the standard trading interfaces of these organizations might be intimidating to novice investors, they also provide user-friendly and simple buying choices.

The flexibility of use comes down to the fact that beginner-friendly choices charge much more than each platform's conventional trading interface to acquire the same coin. Before making your first crypto buy, or not long after, you may want to learn enough to use the traditional trading platforms to save money.

As a beginner to crypto, verify that the exchange or brokerage of your choice allows US dollar transfers and purchases. Many cryptocurrency exchanges can't buy cryptocurrency directly with another cryptocurrency. As a result, you'll have to go via a different exchange to get the tokens you need.

Cryptocurrency Broker

By communicating with exchanges on your behalf and providing clear user interfaces, brokers make the process of purchasing cryptocurrencies easier. Some levy costs are much greater than the fees charged by exchanges. Many "free" brokers make money by selling information about your transactions to major brokerages or funds or by not carrying out your business at the best available market pricing, both of which are deceptive trade practices. Two of the best-known cryptocurrency brokers are Robinhood and SoFi.

Digital wallets may not seem like a huge problem, but advanced crypto investors prefer to keep their currencies in them. Even though brokers are undeniably convenient, you need to be informed that transferring your bitcoin off the site may be difficult. You cannot withdraw any of your crypto assets while utilizing Robinhood or SoFi, for example. Some cryptocurrency users opt for offline, non-internet-connected hardware wallets for an extra layer of protection.

Here are the steps you should follow:

Create an Account and Verify It

Preventing fraud and complying with federal regulations necessitates taking this step. Signing up for an account with a cryptocurrency broker or exchange is easy after you've decided on one. You may have to prove your identification depending on the platform and the amount you want to purchase. When the verification procedure is complete, you may not be able to do so to buy or sell any cryptocurrency. Even a selfie may be required to verify that the papers you provide match your look on the site, which may need your driver's license or passport.

Make a Cash Deposit to Invest

You'll need to have money in your account before purchasing cryptocurrency. If you're using a debit or credit card, you may make a payment by connecting your account to your crypto wallet and requesting a wire transfer. You may have to wait a few days to use the money you deposit for certain exchanges and brokers to buy cryptocurrencies.

One word of caution before you buy: While you may deposit money with a credit card at certain exchanges or brokers, doing so is exceedingly risky—and costly. As cash advances, credit card issuers accept cryptocurrency transactions made with a credit card. As a result, you'll pay more excellent interest rates and extra cash advance costs than you would on everyday purchases. When you take out a cash advance, you may be charged a fee of 5% of the transaction amount. Assuming that your crypto exchange or brokerage charges costs of up to 5%, this means you might lose 10% of your crypto buy to fees.

Submit a Cryptocurrency Order

A bitcoin order may be placed as soon as the funds in your account are available. Cryptocurrencies like Bitcoin and Ethereum are well-known, but there are other less prominent coins like Theta Fuel and Holo.

You may enter the ticker symbol (Bitcoin is BTC, for example) and the number of coins you wish to purchase when picking which cryptocurrency to buy. A fractional share of high-priced tokens like Bitcoin or Ethereum may be bought on most cryptocurrency exchanges and brokers.

Cryptocurrencies with the highest market capitalization are listed below, they are subject to variation:

- Bitcoin (BTC)

- Ethereum (ETH)

- Tether (USDT)

- USD Coin (USDC)

- BNB (BNB)

- XRP (XRP)

- Cardano (ADA)

- Solana (SOL)

- Binance USD (BUSD)

- Polkadot (DOT)

Choose a Storage Method

Money worth millions of dollars in Bitcoin is already gone because people forgot or lost the codes to their accounts. As a result, cryptocurrency exchanges are vulnerable to hacking and theft since they are not insured by the Federal Deposit Insurance Corporation (FDIC). That's why having a safe location to store your cryptocurrency is so crucial.

To reiterate, you may have little to no control over how your bitcoin is held if you acquire it via a broker. More possibilities are available if you buy cryptocurrencies on an exchange.

As soon as you purchase a cryptocurrency, it is generally kept on the exchange in a "crypto wallet." A hot or cold wallet is a good alternative. If you don't trust the service, your exchange utilizes or wants to keep it out of the public eye. A minor charge may be required depending on the exchange and the amount of money you are transferring.

Hot Wallets

These are online crypto wallets that can be accessed from any Internet-enabled device, including smartphones, tablets, and laptops because they're still linked to the Internet and pose a more significant theft risk.

If you are locked out of your hot wallet, custodians can assist you in getting back into your account.

Cold Wallets

Because they are not linked to the Internet, cold crypto wallets are the safest way to store your bitcoin. A USB flash drive or a hard disc is one example of an external storage device.

If you misplace the device's keycode or it malfunctions, you may never be able to retrieve your bitcoin.

Buying Cryptocurrency in Other Ways

At the moment, purchasing cryptocurrency seems like a good investment idea, but it comes with a lot of volatility and danger. Here are a few alternatives to using an exchange or a broker to invest in Bitcoin or other cryptocurrencies:

Anticipate the Crypto Exchange-Traded Funds (ETFs)

Exchange-traded funds (ETFs) are a popular investment vehicle that provides you access to hundreds of different assets at once. Because of this, they are less hazardous than investing in individual assets and offer rapid diversification.

Many people are eager for Bitcoin ETFs, which enable investors to invest in many cryptocurrencies at once. There are currently no cryptocurrency ETFs accessible to the general public, but this might change soon. Kryptcoin, VanEck, and WisdomTree have applied for three cryptocurrency ETFs to be reviewed by the US Securities and Exchange Commission (SEC) as of June 2021.

Invest in Companies Connected to Cryptocurrency

To get a taste of the cryptocurrency market, you may want to explore investing in firms that utilize or own cryptocurrency and the blockchain that supports it. Governed oversight is in place. As an example of a publicly listed corporation in which to invest, consider:

- **Nvidia (NVDA).** Mining cryptocurrencies relies on graphics processing units (GPUs), which this technological business manufactures and sells.

- **PayPal (PYPL).** In addition to purchasing goods and services online or sending money to loved ones, this payment network just included the ability to buy and sell various cryptocurrencies using PayPal and Venmo accounts.

- **Square (SQ).** People may now purchase, trade, and store cryptocurrencies with Square's Cash App. More than $220 million has been spent by a small-business payment service provider since October 2020 on Bitcoin purchases. The company revealed in February 2021 that Bitcoin accounted for almost 5% of its total cash on hand.

It's essential to consider your long-term financial objectives and present financial condition before investing in cryptocurrencies or cryptocurrency-related firms. One tweet may send the price of cryptocurrency plunging, making it a hazardous investment. As a result, funding should be approached with prudence and caution.

Crypto Wallets

Using a wallet is the most secure method of storing your Bitcoin. Hosted wallets, non-custodial wallets, and hardware wallets are the most common forms of crypto wallets. The appropriate cryptocurrency for you will depend on your goals and desired level of security.

Hosted Wallets

Hosted wallets are the most popular and easy-to-use crypto wallets. It's termed "hosted" because a third party manages your crypto assets on your behalf, just as a bank does with your cash. On Coinbase, for example, your cryptocurrency is stored in a hosted wallet. If you've ever heard of somebody "dropping their keys" or "missing their USB wallet," you don't have to worry about that with a hosted wallet.

Keeping your cryptocurrency in an online wallet means you won't lose it if you misplace your password. A downside to using a hosted wallet is that you can't use all of the features of crypto. When it comes to hosted wallets, though, this may alter.

Hosted Wallets: How to Get Started

- **Pick a reliable platform.** You must focus on three things: security, usability, and adherence to legal and financial mandates.

- **Open an account.** Choose a strong password and enter your personal information. Using two-step verification provides an additional degree of security (2FA).

- **Purchase cryptocurrencies or make a transfer of them.** It is possible to acquire cryptocurrency using a bank account or credit card on most crypto platforms and exchanges. Hosted wallets may be used to store any cryptocurrency that you currently hold.

Self-Custody Wallets

An independent wallet like Coinbase Wallet or MetaMask gives you complete control over your coins. Non-custodial wallets don't depend on a third party to protect your coin. While they supply the software to store your crypto, you are alone responsible for remembering and protecting your password. You can't access your crypto if you lose or forget your password (also called a "private key" or "seed phrase"). Anyone with your private key may access your assets.

In a non-custodial wallet, you can access complex crypto activities like yield farming, staking, lending, borrowing, and more. A hosted wallet is the simplest way to buy, sell, send, and receive bitcoin.

Creating a Non-Custodial Cryptocurrency Wallet

- **Get a wallet app.** Such as:

- **BRD** is an open-source wallet with its base in Zurich, it is possible to use with iOS and Android devices. Offer a strong security system. Run with BTC, ETH, BCH, XRP, and ERC-20, it is possible to buy cryptocurrency by many fiat currencies.

- **Coinomi** has very stringent security features, works with Android, iOS, Linus, macOS, and Windows, offers multilanguage support, and supports more than 120 networks and hundreds of digital assets, it is possible to make transfers of crypto through SegWit to have lighter transactions.

- **Edge** for mobile with Android and IOD devices, you can exchange fiat with crypto.

- **Exodus** is the right choice for beginners, easy and developed to run with Linux, Mac, Windows, and devices with Android and iOS systems. Supports cryptocurrencies such as BTC, ETH, BNB, SOL, and about 125 others. If you make direct crypto-to-crypto purchases, Exodus pays a percentage of the profit that will be deposited directly into the account.

- **Coinbase Wallet** supports EVM-compatible blockchain, Ethereum, token Solana and SPL are mobile-friendly with the app, fast to use, and permits to hold in the wallet Bitcoin, Dogecoin, Litecoin, Ripple, and more. Actually do not require any registration or KYC.

- **MetaMask** is very popular, it works in many protocols such as DeFi, and NFT, work in different ways, for example, on ERC-20, EVM networks, see Arbitrum BNB Chain, Optimism, Polygon, and more, does not permit saving BTC or SOL, in any case, all cryptocurrencies that are not on EVM platform.

- **MyEtherWallet** is open source, a bit technical, easy to use, works with Ethereum blockchain, supports BNB, ETC, Polygon, and more.

- **Trust Wallet** was purchased by Binance in 2018. Supports over 35 blockchains and many digital assets. This wallet works with dApps on Ethereum and other EVM systems, this does not compromise security.

- **Open an account.** Unlike a hosted wallet, a non-custodial wallet requires no personal information. Not even an email.

- **Note your secret key.** It's a 12/24-word sentence. Please keep it safe. You can't access your crypto if you lose or forget this 12/24-word phrase.

- **Wallet crypto transfer.** Buying crypto using fiat currency (such as dollars or euros) isn't always available, so you'll need to move crypto into your non-custodial wallet from somewhere.

Customers of Coinbase may choose between a hosted and self-custody wallet. The Coinbase app is a hosted wallet. You may also use the Coinbase wallet standalone app to benefit from a non-custodial wallet. It's simple to acquire crypto using regular cash and engage in sophisticated crypto activities for our consumers. Ether wallet setup is free.

Hardware Wallets

Hardware wallets, which are more complicated and expensive, offer certain advantages, like the ability to keep your cryptocurrency safe even if your computer is compromised. Using a hardware wallet, the private keys to your cryptocurrency are saved on a device the size of a thumb drive. As a result, these devices are more challenging to use than software wallets, and they may cost as much as $100 to purchase.

Hardware wallet setup instructions:

- **Buy the hardware.** It's hard to go wrong with either Ledger or Trezor (safe deposit). Some other hardware are Bitbox, Cold Card, and KeepKey.

    Before buying hardware research all the information you need for your activity.

- **Activate the software.** Wallets may be set up with different software for each brand. Create your wallet by downloading the software from the company's website and following the instructions.

- **Transfer crypto to your wallet.** Cryptocurrency may be stored in various places, much like cash (in a bank account, a safe, or even beneath the mattress). When it comes to cryptocurrency, the choice is yours. You may use a hosted wallet to make things easy, you can use a non-custodial wallet to have complete control over your crypto, or you can use a hardware wallet to be extra cautious.

    To acquire crypto using conventional currencies (US dollars or euros), you need to change fiat into crypto and deposit it into your wallet.

CHAPTER 13

CRYPTOCURRENCY TRADING

I s inevitable to insert a chapter dedicated to trading in a text that deals with blockchain and cryptocurrencies. One of the advantages of this technology is that all those who discover it immediately feel the need to begin to understand how the market works. The reasons that push a person to start trading cryptocurrencies can vary. Some do it out of pure curiosity, to better understand the same technology, or simply because they see the possibility of earning money. In any case, it is extremely common that those who approach cryptocurrencies very often decide to open a trading account on an exchange platform.

This has allowed many people to acquire the first rudiments of economic-financial education: a form of education that is almost completely absent in our country and which would be greatly needed. The "quantum" leap that people who start using BTC and other cryptocurrencies make is that since they have full control of their money, they can also freely invest it. And for the rest, as I like to say, "Even a monkey can make a profit by trading." What does this activity consist of? I think one word is enough to say it and that word is "rules." Trading is a system of rules.

What a trader does is take advantage of these value fluctuations to make a profit, buy BTC at a low price (for example at $100) and resell at a higher price (for example at $120); the difference between the selling price and the buying price represents the profit (or loss) realized with that single operation.

In cryptocurrency trading, we can observe two big trends: that of traders who always operate in pairs with a fiat currency (for example, they buy BTC to earn dollars,) and those who trade in cryptocurrencies (they buy any altcoin to earn BTC.) Whoever operates like in the first case (i.e., accumulating dollars) is a person who is probably convinced that the supremacy of fiat currencies will never be scratched by cryptocurrencies, and consequently uses price changes to earn more legal tender currency. Those who instead operate in the second way (i.e., accumulating Bitcoin) are convinced that, regardless of what happens during bearish cycles, BTC is destined in the long term to continue to increase its value, always hitting new peaks.

The most popular trading strategies include:

1. **Scalping:** This means that the trader opens and closes numerous transactions during the same day, aiming to make a profit in the shortest possible time by taking advantage of even the smallest price changes.

2. **Day trading:** In this case the trader tends to make fewer operations, rarely exceeding 2 or 3 in the same day, and as a basic rule each operation is opened and closed strictly within 24 hours.

3. **Swing trading:** Those who do this type of trading reduce the number of transactions even more compared to the day trader, and as a basic rule the duration of the trade is extended from 1 day (maximum duration of day trading) up to 10 days (indicatively the maximum time frame within which the single transaction should be closed.)

4. **Cassettista:** Operates more according to an investment logic than (as in other cases) in purely speculative logic. Between when the drawer opens an operation and when they close it, months can easily pass; moreover, it is difficult for this type of operator to manage more than 2 or 3 investments at the same time.

In general, a good trader knows how to adapt their operations to all four trading styles based on the market trend; therefore depending on the moment the trader decides to adopt one style instead of another, the same trader who today does scalping could then suddenly adopt a swing trading logic, and then go back to scalping once the previous operations are closed.

As we said, trading is basically a system of rules, once these rules are set correctly you inevitably start making a profit; this does not mean that you will easily become a billionaire, but simply that you will be able to make your savings relatively easily. The difficult thing, when we talk about trading, is not even learning the technique (which after all is accessible to anyone), but having full control of one's psychology.

Each trader is constantly exposed to a great psychological pressure that induces them, regardless of the rules they have given themself, to sell or buy unreasonably; the point is that no matter how good you are, all traders are trading at a loss. A good trader simply accumulates more profit than loss. The psychological reactions of each operator can be different and can change, as well as from person to person, from situation to situation; therefore, there are no rules valid for everyone to manage the most demanding aspect (which is the psychological dimension) of the trading activity.

In the next chapters, therefore, in addition to describing the functioning of some fundamental tools in the activity of each trader, we will also try to make more general reflections on this type of profession to offer each reader a broad point of view and a sufficient basis.

How to Read the Graphs

Increasing — Bullish Candle Stick
- High
- Upper shadow
- Close
- Real Body
- Open
- Lower shadow
- Low

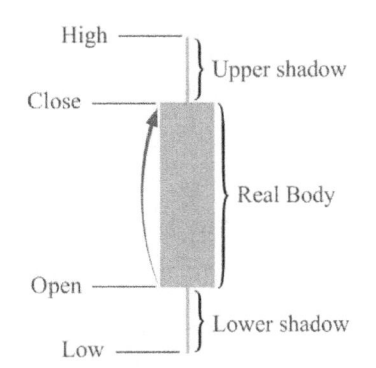

Decreasing — Bearish Candle Stick
- High
- Upper shadow
- Open
- Real Body
- Close
- Lower shadow
- Low

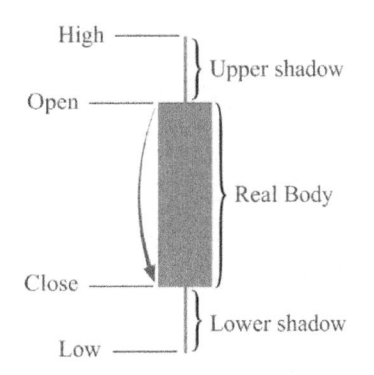

Finding yourself trading when you discover cryptocurrencies is a very common thing, and the fact that those who approach this type of activity do so thinking of becoming immensely rich in record time is, unfortunately, the same. Even if anyone can learn to exploit the market cycles to profit, it is not certain that all those who engage in this activity will reach the goal. As mentioned before, trading is a system of rules, but since we impose these rules on ourselves, many tend to infringe on them. In any case, the first rule that every trader must follow is "never invest more than you are willing to lose."

The first thing we must do is to learn to read stock market charts which, in jargon, are called "Japanese candlestick charts." Obviously, the price trend can also be graphically rendered by a line graph, but the candlestick charts give us much more information than we could obtain by observing a line.

The reason why these graphs are called this is quite intuitive:

the graphic signs (colored red and green) resemble candles. Each candle on the chart expresses the price trend in the unit of time defined by the user. Precisely for this reason, we hear about charts for one hour, four hours, one day, one week, and so on; this is the length of time covered by one candle.

Now, let's imagine reading a 1D (1 day) chart; we know that each candle graphically represents what happened over the last 24h. Therefore, if the candle is colored red this means that in the 24 hours the price has dropped, on the contrary, if the candle is colored green it means that the price has gone up.

The height of the candle represents the change in unit price. When we read a red candle (which signals a price drop in the unit of time) the upper border indicates the opening price, and the lower one the closing price of the session, and vice versa for a green candle.

In some cases, we can observe candles that are not colored and substantially resemble crosses. This type of candle indicates that the opening price was substantially identical to the closing price; the edges of these crosses (directed upwards or downwards) graphically represent the price changes (maximum and minimum) that occurred during the session.

Let's take some practical examples and imagine that the price of 1 BTC after starting from a price of $10 at the opening touched a maximum of $15 and then closed the session at $12. How is all this represented by the candle? Simple, in the meantime, we will have a green candle (because the price has risen), similar to a rectangle whose lower edge is positioned at $10 (the opening) and the upper margin is positioned at $12 (the close); from the upper margin. Then, we will see starting a straight line ("shadow") that reaches $15.

As another example, let's imagine that the opening price is $20 and the closing price is $17, with the day's low at $15 and the day's high at $22; in this case, the candle will be red (session at a loss), the upper margin (opening price) will be positioned at $20, from here the upper shadow (the straight line) will start, which represents the high of the day and will touch share $22, while the lower margin of the candle (closing price) will settle at $17, the level from which the lower shadow (always another straight line) will start and will reach the low of the day at $15.

For the last example, a session that opens and closes at $17, corresponds to the minimum of the day and with a maximum peak reached of $20. In this case, the candle will look like a cross; it will not have any color because the opening and closing price coincide, and there will be no lower shadow because the day's low has never gone below the opening, but there will be a long upper shadow that it will extend up to $20.

Everything that we have illustrated in words up to now can be found summarized in the image below that will allow you to better understand all the new terminology we have introduced.

The Technical Analysis

In these few chapters, we have discussed several fundamental concepts for trading, how to read a candlestick chart, and established that trading means creating your own system of rules. This last aspect is fundamental because, without an effective system of rules, we will never be able to trade effectively.

The purpose of these rules is not just to allow you to make a profit, but rather to allow the trader to ease the psychological pressure to which they will inevitably be exposed until the moment they close the operation, and to establish instead how to realize the profit each operator is based on what is essentially a real "collection of signals."

The first question that every person inevitably asks themselves when they start trading is "what moves the price of a cryptocurrency?" Finding a good answer to this question already means you have taken the first step to become a good trader. The price is mainly driven by two factors: the greed of the market and the news breaking into the market. These two factors, taken together, generate the price movements that allow us to make a profit.

When we begin to operate in a particular market, any news concerning it can trigger a bullish or bearish reaction in the price trend. There is news, such as the possibility of a hard fork or the release of a new version of the platform, which inevitably triggers the rise in prices. Other news, however, can do the exact opposite and sink the value of a coin. For example, the price of crypto may fall if the news spreads that the official wallet of a certain currency is defective or that a certain cryptocurrency is about to be excluded (delisted) from a large platform.

If understanding how and why news moves the market is easy enough, it is more difficult to understand the way in which the greed of operators causes price fluctuations. First of all, what we have to understand is that the price trend is never linear, but more resembles the waves as seen in the above candle charts.

When we begin to imagine the price trend as if it were a wave, we begin to frame two different trends: one short term in which the price moves between minimums and maximums within what is called a "channel," and, at the same time, we find the second trend in progress, more in the long term, which sees the price destined to increase or decrease.

There are obviously several tools available to traders to

recognize these trends in the price (some of which we will get to know later) but in principle, the dynamics we are witnessing are always the same. Since all traders pursue the same goal (making a profit) and all read the same chart at the same time when certain conditions occur all traders will click en masse to take advantage of the opportunity, and here, as mentioned, the greed of the market ends up moving the price.

However, this is also true on the contrary; the fears of the market can cause a wave of sales that can lead the individual trader to suffer significant losses. The ability to read the market trends through the price trend on a chart, and to recognize the moments of reversal (both short and long term) in the main trend, is all classified as "technical analysis." What the trader does, in other words, is to use the tools at their disposal to define the trend of the market and try to make a profit based on technical analysis.

The bad thing about technical analysis is that it is not an exact science, but more of a statistical calculation. None of the data we get from reading the charts ever gives us guarantees; although there are more relevant (and more reliable) signals than others, there are no 100% safe trading signals. Moreover, every good trader naturally oscillates between a speculative approach and a more moderate one based on the investment. Consequently, for a complete operation on the market, technical analysis is not sufficient, but it is always necessary.

All the concepts we are exposing exist in every type of

market; the graphs read the same way both on the forex and the cryptocurrency market, the technical analysis is the same whether you are investing in stocks or buying coins, and fundamental analysis is a concept that always exists.

When we buy shares, for example, the fundamental analysis consists in reading the financial statements of the company we are going to invest in; in the cryptocurrency market, the fundamental analysis is done by collecting information of a different nature, as we saw better before. For now, let's focus on knowing some elementary tools that every trader normally uses in their daily practice to search for trading signals that allow them to make a profit.

Supports and Resistances

We have said that the price moves like a wave within a long-term trend that can be bullish or bearish. Shortly, in a bull market, the price tends to always touch new peaks, while in a bear market it tends to always touch new lows.

When in the middle of a well-defined trend, the price fails to touch a new peak (minimum or maximum.) This is the first sign of a weakening of the trend and indicates that we may be close to a reversal of the main trend.

If we then graphically combine the maximum peaks reached by the price with a straight line and do the same for the minimum peaks, we graphically obtain important levels at the level of technical analysis; these are called support (the line that joins the minimum peaks) and resistance (the line that joins the maximum peaks.)

Therefore, when the price is near a support level, this represents a difficult level to break downwards, and it is easy to say that (in the short-term trend) the price is going to rebound. In the same way, when the price is near the resistance, is easy for the price to begin to slide down, seeking the first useful support again. However, we must always consider that the more times these levels are tested, the less likely it becomes that they can withstand the next wave. When the price starts beating against a resistance, sooner or later it is likely to be able to break it and, therefore, start to rise.

In this dynamic, there are two relevant moments for a trader's activity: when the price is near those price levels that we have called supports and resistances, and when the price breaks these levels. Given that today there are financial instruments that allow you to make a profit even when the price is falling (short sale), it would be preferable for a novice trader to concentrate on making all upward operations and then later integrate more advanced tools into their operations.

Our neophyte crypto trader, who wants to make a profit with the upward variations in the price, has two ideal moments to open a position: precisely when the price is near a support level and when the price breaks a resistance. Opening a position by counting on the rebound near the support is a strategy that often allows you to make a profit, but which presents greater risks since it is not said that the support will hold. Instead, opening the position when the resistance is broken upwards is a more moderate trading strategy that allows us to take fewer risks but offers us fewer profit opportunities.

In any case, despite how sophisticated our market analysis skills are, no one can really predict where the price is going. This is always true, even more so in a market like cryptocurrencies, subject to continuous manipulation. In fact, as the cryptocurrency market is often not very liquid, some operators with large financial capacities are in a position to be able to provoke speculative maneuvers that are referred to as "pump and dump." They accumulate large quantities of coins at a certain price for weeks, and then suddenly inject enormous volumes of liquidity, causing a rise in prices that it will subsequently allow reselling to other operators at a profit.

After completing the speculative maneuver and painfully trimming the package to all the operators who had rushed to chase that sudden rise, the price of the currency (lacking the liquidity that had allowed the rise) falls back down.

Therefore, among the rules that should be given when trading cryptocurrencies, we have the rule of not operating on illiquid pairs (which generate a trading volume lower than a minimum that is commonly established at around 20 BTC per day) and the rule of investing in projects that you know well and in which

OSCAR BUFF

you have great confidence (so you have to study the various platforms, carry out your fundamental analysis, and carefully choose which ones you want to operate on). Before moving on, let's use a simple image to fix what we just said; in the following chart, we clearly see that the price moves within a "channel" limited by two lines that respectively join the minimum peaks (the red support line and the black resistance line.)

When at a certain point the price shows the first sign of weakness and does not show itself capable of going to test the resistance again (black line) here it tries to breathe for some time near the support; at this point, we witness the last attempt at a bullish sortie, then the price suddenly drops, breaks the level (already tested several times previously), crosses the red line (the support), and enters a markedly bearish cycle in which at each new low one that is always lower than the previous one follows.

Relative Strength Index (RSI)

We have said that every trader uses, in their daily operations, a series of tools that help them to analyze the chart they are reading. These instruments can be divided into two broad categories: indicators (which freely replicate the price trend on the chart) and oscillators (which move in a pre-determined range of values). These tools often give us very clear signals of what is happening to the price, and their correct interpretation is often what makes the difference between loss and profit.

The trading signals do not only come from reading the data we get from the indicators and oscillators, but also directly through the price chart by plotting the levels that represent the "supports" and "resistances." Since for each currency pair on which we operate we can change the unit of time (represented graphically by the candles), we have a multiplicity of different signals depending on how we set the time frame.

Regardless of the modality we use to obtain the trading signal, in the meantime we must always start from the assumption that the signal is all the more solid the more the TF is set in an expanded manner; a chart with a 1-week time frame, therefore, offers more solid signals than a chart with a 1-hour time frame.

For example, if we are trading on the BTC-ETH pair, spending BTC to buy ETH. If I wanted to buy ETH spending BTC, what I would do would be to wait for a moment when a trading signal appears on the 1-week chart, start observing the lower TF, then slowly narrow down the TF to find the optimal time to buy. To reduce the risk, therefore, we never rely on a single trading signal, but we go in search of what is called "convergence" of signals. If it is true that "many clues do not prove," it is also true that the more clues you have, the higher the chances of winning your bet. Because in a sense this is what we are doing; we are betting that the price will go up. Among all the tools used by traders, is there one that is simple to understand and that is commonly used and appreciated by the majority of the community? Yes, it's called RSI (relative strength index).

It is an oscillator that moves continuously between a minimum (equal to 0) and a maximum (equal to 100) invented by John Welles Wilder (who illustrated its operation to the public in 1979 with the book "New Concepts in Technical Trading System") and whose purpose is to help the trader identify the points where the strength of the trend is running out; the mathematical formula would help us understand why certain indications are obtained from the RSI. In any case, this does not change the operation, so let's just say that the RSI, moving between a minimum of 0 and a maximum of 100, reaches two bands in which the trader's attention increases: the 0–30 band (which is defined as oversold) and the 70–100 band (which is defined as overbought).

When the RSI crosses the oversold and overbought ranges, it means that the market is in a phase of "excess," in which traders are essentially stubborn to sell and buy beyond reasonable. Unfortunately, to make a profit, it is not enough to rush to buy in the oversold ranges and sell in the overbought ranges, based on the strength of the current trend. The RSI can remain in "extreme" conditions (oversold or overbought) for long periods.

There are particular moments, however, in which anomalies are produced on the RSI if we compare the trend of the oscillator with what we read on the price chart. For example, when we see the price mark a low of $20, rise up to $23, and then return to mark a new low of $17, what we clearly read on the price chart is that by combining the two lows we obtain a descending line. In certain circumstances, however, it happens that in conjunction with the two lows on the price chart, the RSI marks two peaks which, once joined, form an ascending line (which moves upwards).

This kind of anomaly is called "divergence," and is formed not only on the RSI but also on other types of oscillators and indicators (always in the same way). There are basically two types of divergences: the bullish ones (which can be read by drawing a line that connects the minimum peaks) and the bearish ones (which can be read by drawing a line that connects the maximum peaks).

Any kind of divergence we could notice between what we read on the price chart and what is expressed by the oscillator gives us a trading signal. In particular, if in a bull market we notice a divergence in the maximum peaks, we have a sell signal (there is, therefore, the possibility of a trend reversal). If instead it is produced by combining the minimum peaks we have a buy signal.

More technically, we should then distinguish the actual divergences (two increasing peaks in the direction of the trend on the price chart in conjunction with two peaks in the opposite direction to that of the trend traced by the oscillator) from the hidden ones (in which the logic is reversed so the peaks expressed by the price are in the opposite direction to that of the trend, while the oscillator behaves in the opposite way). In the following graph, however, we will analyze only the classic divergences, while we will deal better with hidden divergences in the paragraph dedicated to MACD. The RSI, in principle, offers us the best trading signals through the divergences that occur in the vicinity of the oversold and overbought ranges; such signals are more solid when they emerge on larger TFs.

A bullish divergence, for example, built on a chart with a 1-week TF in a strong oversold situation and near solid support, is almost always a good time to open a long position. The more signals we have that push us to buy, the more naturally we will be prepared to open a position. To simplify all this reasoning, below we graphically illustrate the functioning of two classic divergences (the first bullish and the second bearish); what we see in the green box is that the price on the chart marks 3 new consecutive lows while the RSI at those lows is rising (all of this is graphically expressed by the red line).

As soon as the price breaks, the resistance begins to grow and undergo an increase of about 30%. Immediately after, however, in the black box, we notice that a bearish divergence is formed. On the chart, the price marks 2 new highs, but the line that joins the respective peaks on the RSI (highlighted in red) is clearly descending.

This time, the support is broken and the price starts to fall. In a trader's operations, the orange circles represent the moment in which it would have been advisable to open the position (the first two) and close it (the last two) to optimize profit and reduce any risks. This type of strategy is not infallible, so by working exclusively with the divergences produced by the RSI we will inevitably end up even getting into some bad situations.

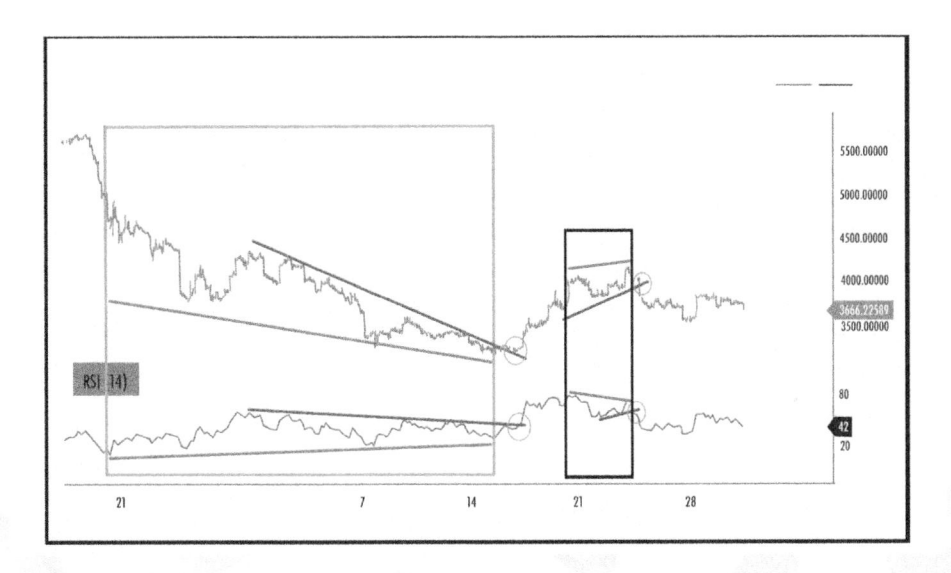

Mobile Media

What we must always have in mind when trading is that each chart offers us all kinds of signals, and it is up to us to interpret

OSCAR BUFF

them correctly by making the different evaluations of the case. When we collect a signal using the RSI, we should go in search of confirmations using different tools to make sure that these also provide us with positive indications.

Among the most useful and simplest tools to integrate into everyday operations, we have the moving averages; these tools only reduce the effect of random peaks by expressing the price trend on the chart in the form of a curve.

There are different types of moving averages; the most commonly used are called simple moving average (SMA or arithmetic average) which assigns the same importance to all the values that the price assumes regardless of whether they are more or less recent; weighted moving average (WMA) which resolves the limit of the SMA by assigning greater relevance to more recent candles; exponential moving average (EMA) which assigns an exponentially increasing value to the most recent price values; and adaptive moving average (AMA, which introduces the analysis of volumes in the calculation necessary to produce the curve that expresses the price trend. Regardless of the type of moving average, the curve that will be represented by the graph will have a different appearance depending on the "period" that we will have set; a 12-period moving average, for example, indicates that each point plotted by the curve represents the average of the last 12 candles.

Moving averages are, therefore, defined as "fast" and "slow" as the reference period increases. In this way, a 12-period moving average (based on the last 12 candles) is considered a fast moving average and a 26-period average (based on the last 26 candles) is considered slow.

Moving averages are important precisely because we can create multiple moving averages with different periods by receiving different indications; in general, the periods most commonly used in technical analysis to plot moving averages are 20, 50, and 100, especially as regards the exponential moving average (which is the one that traders normally use the most). These tools offer us a quick and immediate glance at the market; for example, when the price is above a moving average the trend is considered bullish, and, on the contrary, if it is below it is considered bearish. The trend is also considered as the more marked the higher the period of the moving average above which the price stands.

This is because the moving averages also represent values of supports and resistances; the more solid, the greater the period used to build the moving average itself. Another very useful indication that the moving averages give us is the way they intertwine, which tells us a lot about the future course of the trend. Normally when a faster moving average trims up a slower moving average, that is the time to buy; on the contrary, the cut down is the time to sell.

Let's try to observe everything we said on a chart (precisely a 1D chart of the BTC/XRP pair). Here we have plotted three exponential moving averages at 20 periods (red curve),

OSCAR BUFF

50 periods (blue curve), and 100 periods (black curve) and highlighted (in green and black) two particular moments in the history of the price trend.

Let's look at the first green rectangle; here at a certain point we clearly see the fast moving average (the 20-period one, colored red) cutting up the two slower moving averages. The price immediately falls back, uses one of the slower moving averages as support, and enters a markedly bullish cycle. In the second green box, we see the same dynamics with the price that first marks a big rise and then uses the slower moving average as support and returns to test the same resistance it had tested with the first rise. The development of the situation that we see unfolding in the green box is that either the price will break the short-term resistance (orange line) to then go and test the long-term one again (yellow line) or it will break the three supports represented by the three moving averages and it will fall back into the area of the last low (purple line) where, in all likelihood, it will either attempt a rebound or begin to build a divergence.

In the black squares we observe the same dynamics, but in reverse; in the first black box we can observe how the fast-moving average cuts down the two slower moving averages one after the other with the price that once passed below it will begin to test the EMA100 (exponential moving average at 100 periods, the black curve in our chart) exactly as if it were a resistance.

In the second black box, the same scenario is repeated but with less vigor; the price seems to be trying to gather around the moving averages but, in the end, the bearish cycle prevails and the price touches its minimum peak. Moving averages in general and exponential averages, in particular, are extremely useful in traders' operations, and if integrated into a broader strategy, they provide us with important indications of the possible future trend of the price.

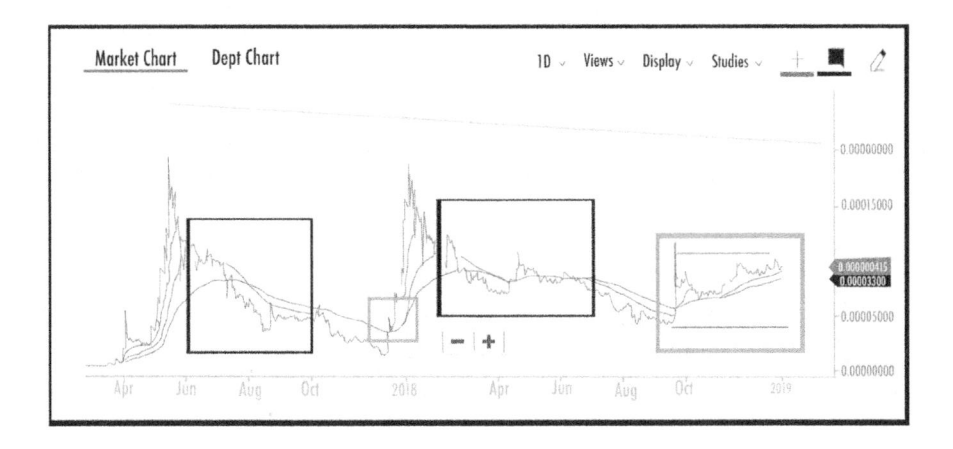

MACD

In the previous chapters, we started introducing the use of tools that should never be missing in a trader's toolbox. This small overview will cover another key tool, the MACD (moving average convergence/divergence.)

The MACD is an indicator considered extremely useful by many traders, who usually integrate it into their operations, built substantially based on data extracted from three different exponential moving averages (at 9, 12, and 26 periods.) One of the main uses of the MACD is to trace differences. Since in the last chapter dedicated to the RSI we dealt with the classic divergences, in this paragraph we will deal specifically with "hidden" divergence. The dynamics with which the divergence is constructed are the same as we have seen previously, so also this time by joining the maximum (or minimum) peaks plotted on the price graph with a straight line, we will notice anomalies (the divergences in fact) concerning what we notice by tracing lines that instead join the peaks constructed by the MACD. The MACD is useful to us because it allows us to obtain more information on the solidity of the trading signal, when in fact we notice the same divergence both on the RSI and on the MACD. This is to be understood as an additional proof of the validity of the signal; the MACD then gives us another interesting starting point, being in fact graphically represented by the trend of two curves, which are substantially two different exponential moving averages (EMA) normally highlighted with blue or black colors (for the slower moving average, at 26 periods) and with red color (for the fastest moving average).

Therefore, when the faster moving average cuts up the slower one we have a bullish signal, and when the slower moving average cuts down the faster one we have a bearish signal. In any case, as we have done in the other paragraphs, we use an image to fix the main concepts.

This time we took two photographs of the market, highlighting them with rectangles (green and black); in the first case (green rectangle) we see a typical hidden bullish divergence, and in the second case (black rectangle) we can see a typically hidden divergence, but this time bearish.

As we can see, the dynamic is identical to the one we described in the paragraph on the RSI, but this time in the green triangle we see that a new low is not marked and that the peak stops at a price slightly higher than that reached in the previous minimum so that the line joining the two peaks (colored blue) is ascending. We find our beautiful hidden divergence by joining the minimums constructed by the MACD and obtaining a new line (also drawn in blue) which instead moves in the opposite direction (descending). The final outcome, regardless of whether the divergence is hidden or not, is the same: the price starts to rise and goes to retest the maximum peak reached previously.

In the black rectangle, we are instead witnessing a bearish scenario. Also, this time the second peak fails to overcome the previous one, but stops a little earlier, so much so that the straight line (blue) that we trace by joining the two peaks is descending; on the MACD, we find our hidden divergence, joining the maximum peaks. In fact, our usual blue line this time is ascending.

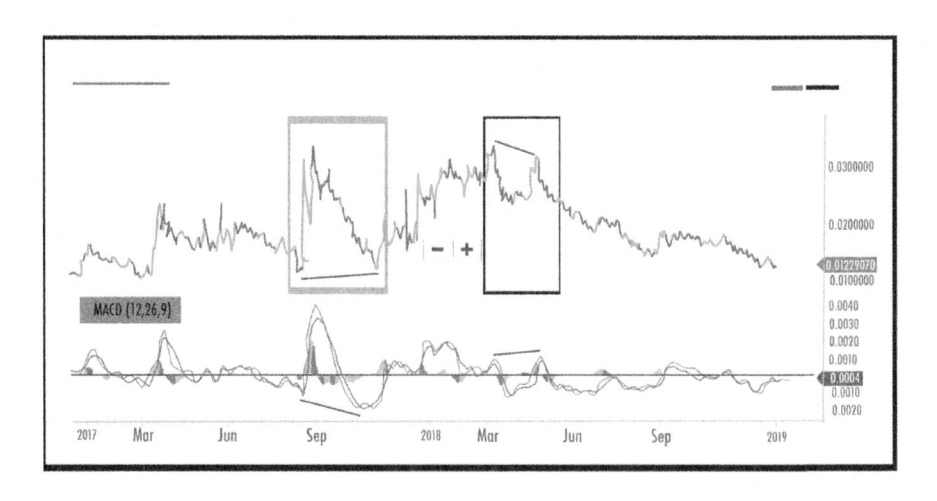

The Analysis Basic in Market of the Cryptocurrencies

In the last few chapters, we have introduced some tools commonly considered essential to start trading. We also explained that there are still many other important tools to know how to use, beyond the scope of this text.

We also had the opportunity to explain that a valid trading strategy does not necessarily have to be extremely complicated, but can be extremely simple as long as it is based on rules. Therefore, a trading strategy is not limited to the tools used for technical analysis, but also includes all those rules that the trader imposes himself intending to manage the pressures in the best possible way.

Let's imagine we bought some coins that we don't really know anything about based on simple technical analysis at a price of $10, and we find ourselves 24 hours later with the same coins which dropped to $8. How would we manage the loss? What would happen is that the doubt of having invested in a dying, useless project or on the usual inevitable package would become an exhausting worm that would push us to sell; perhaps in the middle of a dump, perhaps at the lowest possible price (with the greatest possible damage.) It happens more frequently than you might imagine.

If, on the other hand, we had bought some coins that we know well, having analyzed in detail the project on which we invested our money, then enduring a collapse from $10 to $8 becomes easier. However good a trader can be in technical analysis, without fundamental analysis it becomes difficult to trade cryptocurrencies. We have already had the opportunity to explain that in the stock market, fundamental analysis can be understood as the collection of information by reading the company's financial statements, but it is a pity that when we talk about cryptocurrencies most of the time there is no company at all, let alone a budget.

However, there are factors that we can take into consideration, such as market capitalization (market cap). By capitalization of a cryptocurrency, we simply mean the total amount that we obtain by multiplying the number of coins in circulation by the value of those coins. Another evaluation that we must make in this sense is then to distinguish the maximum supply (21 million coins, for example, if we are talking about BTC) from that available (circulating). Today, there are about 19,5 million BTC in circulation, compared to a maximum number of coins that will ever end up on the market equal to 21 million.

The quantity of coins in circulation, in relation to the maximum number of coins that the network has budgeted, is one of the factors that we should study for a new cryptocurrency. For a real fundamental analysis, we should be able to disassemble the code of the open-source platform and understand how it is made, how it works, and above all if it is well done. There are not many people who have the skills to do a true fundamental analysis of a blockchain project and who know how to "disassemble" the platform and understand how it works. Therefore, ordinary people, who do not have great computer skills, have other ways to try to understand if a project can be trusted or not.

The very first things that every cryptocurrency trader wants to know when investing their money are about the community (the nodes and users in the network) and the identity of the people involved in developing the project. When we are faced with a coin that is spent by thousands of people every day and processed by its own blockchain through a sufficiently large and decentralized network of nodes, we are already moderately sure that we are dealing with a good starting material.

But there are other details that we are interested in knowing, especially concerning the team of developers that takes care of carrying out the project. Each cryptocurrency should have its own official website and, within the official website, there must necessarily be a section in which the leading figures within the community are mentioned. If there is a company or nonprofit behind a project, then figures such as the CEO, department heads, and other executives should also be indicated.

If, on the other hand, there is neither a company nor a foundation behind a project, then on the website there should be a shred of the "about us" section in which the developers are mentioned. What we need to understand is who are the people most exposed in the project: if they are serious people, if they are established, esteemed, or not. In short, the more we know the better.

Obviously, even the project led by a good, brilliant, and capable person can end up shipwrecked, and even "famous" people can throw a package at you. But in general, the quality of any project is always closely linked to the quality of the people who take care of it. If we have a decentralized network worthy of the name, with thousands of users who spend that cryptocurrency every day, and a team of developers known and respected internationally, then we have a whole series of signals that are very useful for building that indispensable trust for us to trade in that particular project.

However, all this is not enough. It is necessary to know the project in more depth, understand how it works, and what kind of opportunities it is capable of offering. To do this, you start by reading its white paper—a document that all the teams disseminate and update periodically, in which all the characteristics and peculiarities of the project should be reported, and it should describe in detail how the technology works.

The white paper should be understood more as advertising brochures than as information documents (after all, no one would ever put pen to paper that their project is useless, does not work, or has no future). From reading them we can still obtain useful information; if a certain currency, for example, uses a consensus protocol that you already know and do not trust, then it will make little sense to invest in that cryptocurrency.

If I find that the ambition of this new coin that I want to invest in is simply to be yet another blockchain-based payment system, I will probably think that there are older and more reliable coins to keep an eye on and that I am not interested in investing my money on what appears to be only the millionth copy of true innovation.

Again, if I discover that the platform on which I want to invest, which on paper offers dozens of very interesting services (from the creation of new tokens to the management of smart contracts), is still far behind the other platforms that preside over the same segment of the market, then I will probably be inclined to want to wait a little longer before investing.

Based on all this information we collect and the different evaluations that each time directly derive from each different information collected, we develop our conviction about a particular project, we define which coins we trust most and which least, with which we feel comfortable operating and which ones we prefer not to deal with.

Of the thousand cryptocurrencies available on the market (without counting the tokens), it will be enough to isolate 20 of those we like best and concentrate on looking for our trading signals for only those 20. Even so, we must understand that fundamental analysis is something that must be carried out daily, and includes all the information and activities that we have to do practically every day.

Since news moves the market, arriving first on news means taking advantage of other traders; to do this, there are a series of very useful operations to do, such as following the developer accounts on social networks, subscribing to the official newsletters, the telegram channel, or participating in discussions on the forums where the community meets. In short, any channel that can provide us with news in advance of other traders must be opened and probed frequently.

Once you have defined a group of cryptocurrencies that you trust, studied their charts, collected information on the technology and the people leading the project, and are ready to intercept any new news and have your own trading strategy made up of precise rules, then you will have all the tools that will allow you to trade cryptocurrencies profitably.

CHAPTER 14

INITIAL COIN OFFERINGS (ICOS)

Have you ever thought of beginning your crypto project, but don't know where to get funding? This could be a colossal dream, but it's achievable. All you need is a plan and the drive to pursue it. Iron it out into a plausible project by outlining a white paper and creating a prototype. Come up with the best strategic marketing campaign and make an Initial Coin Offering (ICO). Who knows if you'll build a better version of Bitcoin or Ethereum?

Initial Coin Offering (ICO) has drawn attention to blockchain startups as a feasible way to raise capital. ICO is Initial Public Offering (IPO) and crowdfunding rolled into one. As crowdfunding, ICOs allow companies to raise money faster and with fewer hassles. If properly designed and executed, ICOs can let you build your business quickly. However, there are caveats. If ICOs are not properly designed, marketed, and executed, your ICO may likely fail to take off.

This chapter will help you explore ICOs so you'll have an idea of how startups, organizations, and businesses make a successful take-off even with low capitalization. You'll be going over some key features of a successful ICO, the process of designing an effective ICO, and some pros and cons of ICO.

Initial Coin Offering Defined

An ICO is an activity for raising capital in the cryptocurrency and blockchain ecosystem. It is similar to IPOs for stocks but the two have important distinctions.

ICOs can provide capital if there are enough people to back up one's business plan. Investors can come from anywhere because of fewer restrictions. You must understand though that this venture is risky because of its high failure rate. ICO is not regulated, and this is the reason why some fundraisers can succumb to inappropriate behavior that may lead to the failure of the ICO.

Despite its high failure rate, ICO remains tempting. Since its inception in 2017 through the ingenuity of Satoshi Nakomoto, ICO has become an alternative to the traditional methods of raising capital.

Purposes of ICOs

There are two main purposes for conducting ICOs. These are:

- To create and introduce new crypto coins that are different from Bitcoin.

- To introduce a new crypto token.

Tokens come in a wide array. They can be traded. They're either classified into investment tokens or utility tokens. Investment tokens are either used in equity, dividend, or voting. On the other hand, utility tokens are for membership, service, and pre-order. Don't get muddled with tokens and cryptocurrencies. Tokens are variations of cryptocurrencies.

Benefits of ICOs

There are many benefits of ICOs for business owners who like to start or grow their business. Let's tackle some of these advantages:

- **Tokens are for everyone.** Anyone who has access to the Internet can join the ICO, unlike IPO which requires accredited investors only with over $1 million net worth. There are no limitations as to who can take part in the ICO.

- **Tokens can be sold in the global market.** ICO gives global investors the chance to invest in new cryptocurrencies. Upon the sale of tokens in ICO, tokens already possess a value.

- **There's less barrier to entry.** Most ICOs are done digitally so investors all around the globe can raise funds from wherever they are located and from whoever they want.

- **There's instant buy-in.** There's a fast, simple, and efficient transaction in buying cryptocurrencies.

Successes in ICOs

- Ethereum was able to raise US$18.5 M on capital.

- ICONOMI was able to raise US$9.1 M on capital.

- Maidsafe Coin was able to generate US$7 M on capital.

- The Golem Project raised US$8.6 M on capital within just 3 hours.

ICO Smart Contract

When tokens are owned, token owners do not become part of the company, so they'll execute a smart contract with the company. An ICO smart contract is an agreement between the company and the investor. The agreement will last for a specific duration and its value is fixed during the entire duration. To make ICO smart contracts legal, they must be made in the blockchain.

Types of ICOs

Before finalizing your ICO smart contract, you've got to choose the type of ICO you want. These are:

- **Private ICOs:** Private ICOs are exclusive to credible investors such as high net worth individuals and financial institutions. Private ICOs are preferred over public offerings.

- **Public ICOs:** Public ICOs are for everybody who wants to invest. This democratized nature makes the public get involved in investment.

How ICO Works

In ICO, cryptocurrencies are offered to interested individuals. Before the offer, several steps must be undertaken, such as:

Preparing a White Paper

A white paper is a document that gives the details on how your idea will work. It contains details such as the number and price of digital tokens that the company plans to sell, the sales period, the sales cap, and other important details. The white paper must contain the project's goal, features, roadmap, team members, financial basics, and the value of the tokens. A white paper usually takes 15 to 20 pages.

The fundraisers may or may not have a prototype to show potential buyers.

Creating Your Tokens

When preparing the tokens, consider the token's name, ticker symbol, the price of the token, number of tokens for sale during the ICO, percentage of tokens held by organizers, bounty cap, and many more. Tokens are created through a platform in the blockchain.

Undertaking Marketing Strategies

Creating a marketing strategy is an excellent way to attract potential investors. You may want to create a website for your project. After all, putting up a website gives an impression of the legitimacy of your ICO. Keep in my mind that your website is the first place that possible investors will start their research.

It would be best if you network with other industries. Establish relationships whenever you can. Start with LinkedIn. They've got tools like Linked Helper, a valuable tool to reach out to potential sponsors and influencers on LinkedIn.

You can also maximize the use of social media like Facebook, Instagram, and Twitter. Don't simply post announcements, be there to respond to questions and comments. It's essential to have a press release. Many cryptocurrency websites are constantly scouting for new projects to feature.

Buying and Selling of Tokens

After all the marketing campaigns, the buying and selling take place. The company now established an exchange of investors for tokens. The nature of the arrangement for tokens is bilateral and is not issued in terms of security/certificate. The token is used as an electronic asset.

Initial Coin Offering vs Initial Public Offering

ICO and IPO share the common objective of fundraising, but they differ in four aspects: regulations, ownership and utility, time for market launch, and defining a company's credibility.

Regulations for Crowdfunding

If ICO is to the white paper, IPO is to the prospectus. Startups for IPOs need to prepare a prospectus—a document that highlights the reasons for offering the stocks to the public and the details that lay down guidelines on how to maintain transparency between the startups and the investors. A prospectus must contain company information, IPO details, risk factors, financial stability of the company, IPO leaders, and key stakeholders of the company.

On the other hand, an ICO does not have a prospectus. What is required is a white paper detailing the project. There's no specific standard for a white paper, unlike a prospectus. The sole aim of a white paper is to inform prospective investors about the project, the tokens offered, and how these tokens can be redeemed.

Laying Down the Company's Credibility

There are a lot of legal requirements for IPOs. This includes a good market reputation, verification of accounts, capitalization, trading permission, and many more. All these requirements vouch for the credibility of the company.

ICOs don't have these standards for regulation except for the white paper. This makes it hard for ICOs to prosper. The white paper isn't really enough to entice investors. Therefore, it's important to back the white paper with a functional prototype. This way, prospect investors will have a clearer understanding of the whole project.

Ownership and Utilization

When you buy a company's stocks, you are in a way securing ownership of the anticipated earnings of the company. Investors can realize their profits when they buy stocks. ICOs do not operate this way. ICOs do not grant ownership in the project but a token is offered. The tokens can be used later for digital transactions.

Time to Launch Market

Processing an IPO is difficult and lengthy. The approval of the IPO from regulating bodies usually takes 4 to 6 months. ICOs take a shorter time to launch because of the lack of regulation. However, it takes time to lure companies to invest. Once a white paper is released and the tokens developed, ICOs will then be issued to the investors.

Pros and Cons of ICOs

Just like a coin that has two sides, ICOs have both advantages and disadvantages.

Advantages of ICOs

ICOs provide opportunities to a lot of startups with promising projects. Just think of what Ethereum has established through these years.

- ICOs produce huge financial returns.

- ICOs increase liquidity.

- ICOs don't require a lot of unnecessary papers.

- ICOs promote the building of community support.

- Incentives are given in exchange for innovation.

- The government doesn't intervene.

Disadvantages of ICOs

- ICOs can be used by scammers. There are less stringent rules in ICOs, so scammers take this chance to victimize people.

- ICOs are sometimes based on mere speculation. The fact that some ICOs are just backed by a white paper makes ICOs hardly believable. Unless there's a functional prototype already built to present to investors.

- There's damage to the company's reputation if the ICO fails. Once a reputation is damaged, it is not easy to rebuild. Honesty and transparency are the two things that can guarantee trust and confidence from your investors.

- There are no regulations. Since ICOs are still new, there are few protocols in place to protect the interests of investors.

- The government doesn't intervene. ICOs are beyond the reach of the government; there are no difficult and lengthy procedures to go through in obtaining permits.

How to Spot an ICO Scam

An ICO is most likely a scam when the company behind it is not transparent regarding its founders and employees. You can also easily spot a scamming ICO through goals that are unrealistic and vague, or if they fail to offer an escrow wallet. An escrow wallet provides investors with an additional layer of security.

Scouting for the Best ICO Launching Service Company

Launching an ICO can be a daunting experience. To save you from the burden of preparing everything, you may consider going with an ICO launching service provider. When you employ the service of an ICO launching service provider, consider the quality of service and customer support that's included in the package. Check for the company's team of experts who possess in-depth experience in blockchain technology and its functionalities.

You must also find out if the company has established an effective and efficient work commitment to their client's ICO project. Ensure that the company integrates a high-end security system in the ICO network. The company must show its support for all phases of ICO development. You need to check on the privacy and security policy of the company, too.

CHAPTER 15

DeFi, dApps, and Non-Fungible Tokens

Decentralized finance (DeFi) has been gaining popularity in the crypto market lately. It's a broad term that covers decentralized money markets, decentralized insurance, decentralized lending, and other decentralized money services.

DeFi, in a sense, is a virtual banking platform that utilizes smart contacts on a blockchain. There are no owners and no controllers.

What's DeFi?

DeFi is a term coined to refer to virtual financial services that have no central authority. Users don't need to deal with banks, brokers, and trading exchange markets. How does it work?

DeFi operates using applications called dApps. DApps provide services like decentralized exchanges (DEXs), gaming, lending, margin trading, P2P transfer, tokenization, staking, and many more.

The dApps are downloadable. They can also be accessed through web-based extensions.

Three Main Types of DeFi

While there are a lot of services offered by DeFis, there are three main categories of DeFi products.

Decentralized Exchanges (DEXs)

DEXs are the first DeFi protocols to be introduced. They were popular even before the term DeFi made it to the headlines in 2020. DEXs facilitate the exchange of one crypto asset to another without disclosing the users' identities. Most DEXs operate on the Ethereum blockchain as this supports the utilization of smart contracts.

Yield Farming Tools

DeFi can also be used as a means of earning passive income called "farm yield." To do this, investors lock their assets and earn from their share of DeFi transaction fees and bonuses.

Lending/Borrowing

Borrowers can use their tokens as collateral to obtain a loan. Lending and borrowing can take place in two ways. There's the centralized finance institution like BlockFi and there's the decentralized finance protocol like Aave. BlockFi is considered a non-bank lending institution that offers loans in US dollars backed by crypto assets. The loan interest starts at 4.5% and has a 12-month duration. Actual interests are based on the amount of the loan. For decentralized finance systems, lenders have to pool their cryptos in the money market. They do this via smart contracts which serve as digital intermediaries. Smart contracts make the coins available to borrowers. Once the coins are released to the borrowers, the smart contract issues interest tokens to the lender. These tokens can be redeemed in exchange for one's underlying asset.

Advantages of DeFi

DeFi is built on a blockchain platform and carries with them the outstanding features of blockchain technology. These are:

- **Open to all.** The decentralization nature of blockchain and DeFi provide equal opportunity for everyone to participate. There's no censorship. There are no requirements as to race, age, or gender. Everyone can access and utilize DeFi regardless of their social background.

- **Automatic and fast transactions.** There is no clearing time or intermediaries. Transactions can take about a couple of minutes, giving you ease and convenience. When you need a loan, you don't have to go to the bank and process so many unnecessary papers.

- **Low-cost transaction.** DeFi offers reasonable transaction fees.

- **No human errors.** Smart contracts eliminate human error and mismanagement.

- **Permissionless.** You don't need to ask for any approval if you want to withdraw or make transfers unlike in the traditional banking system which requires many procedures and paperwork.

Disadvantages of DeFi

Since DeFi is built on the Ethereum blockchain platform, the disadvantages are similar to that of the blockchain technology too.

- **Uncertainty.** There's no certainty about the future of the Ethereum blockchain as it is still changing. The same uncertainty is inherited by DeFi for being a secondary technology built on blockchain.

- **Scalability.** The Ethereum blockchain, at full capacity, can only process 13 transactions per second.

- **Problems with smart contracts.** Smart contracts are vulnerable to hacking. A slight alteration in the codes can lead to a loss of funds.

- **High collateral.** When the value of crypto assets at stake is high, DeFi requires a high value of collaterals to cover risks.

- **Low interoperability.** Interoperability enables blockchains to interact with one another. However, this operation is highly complicated considering that there are different types of blockchains like Bitcoin, Ethereum, Binance, etc., each having its own DeFi system.

What Are dApps?

Decentralized applications (dApps) are decentralized applications that are run on a blockchain platform. They're similar to normal applications and have similar functions. The difference is that they're run on a P2P network.

Key Features of dApps

DApps have these notable features:

- The dApps are open-source and they operate on their own without any central authority.

- The data and records are open to the public.

- They use cryptography to secure the network.

What Are Non-Fungible Tokens?

Would you believe that digital artist Beeple sold his work at an auction for $69 million?

There's nothing like an explosion of crypto or blockchain news that can leave you wondering "what's all the fuss about?" You might be out of touch, but here's what you've been missing.

Non-fungible tokens (NFTs) are selling for enormous prices, just like Beeple's work of art depicting an image of a naked Donald Trump.

NFTs are authentic digital assets that are certified on a blockchain ledger. They're memorabilia or collectibles. The term "non-fungible" means something unique or one of a kind. Although NFTs use blockchain technology, they're different from cryptocurrencies like Bitcoin and Ether. Each NFT is identifiable with its own role and value and is defined by metadata. Almost anything can become an NFT: a piece of art or even a tweet.

Yes, NFTs are artwork that can be stored in digital files and then easily duplicated.

NFTs cannot be readily exchanged for another token. They're sold on exchanges but not traded. They're not a mode of exchange for purchases, unlike cryptocurrencies.

Society is slowly transitioning from physical media to virtual experiences, with young people taking the lead in buying digital collectibles as a store for value. These NFTs are revolutionizing copyright control too.

Pros and Cons of NFTs

Pros

- NFTs are unique so it's difficult to counterfeit them.

- NFTs are scarce as the creator can limit the number to be circulated.

- NFTs are verifiable on the blockchain.

- NFTs can be easily transferred via secondary markets.

- NFTs are a good avenue for creatives to get the value

for their work online.

- NFTs can be equated with having physical collectibles or memorabilia.

Cons

- There are always online risks like false advertising and counterfeiting.

- NFTs are expensive.

- NFTs can be confused with cryptos.

Popular NFTs in the Market

There's an increasing number of NFTs available in the market. Here's a list of the prevailing NFTs in the global crypto market:

- CryptoKitties

- Sorare

- OpenSea

- NFT Yourself

- Waifus

- Rarible

- Axie Infinity

- Async.art

- POW NFT

- Hashmasks

What Are NFTs For?

What do you need NFTs for? Are they only for collectibles?

NFTs can be used in the following:

- Gaming

- Art tokenization

- Lending platforms

- Music and video

- Fashion

- Digital assets

- Real estate

How to Buy NFTs?

You can purchase NFTs on various platforms, like a P2P blockchain or in an NFT marketplace like Rarible. When using Rarible, follow these steps:

1. Create a digital wallet.

2. Fund your wallet.

3. Connect your wallet to Rarible.

4. Look for an item you like at Rarible.

5. Click to "Buy."

6. Authorize the payment via the wallet prompt.

How to Create NFTs?

It's easy to make your own NFT:

1. Create your wallet.

2. Connect your wallet to the NFT marketplace.

3. Sign in to the NFT marketplace e.g., Rarible.

4. Create a collectible.

5. Add details like title, creator, owner, price, and a short description.

6. Authorize payment for minting fees.

7. List your NFT on the marketplace.

The picture below shows an example of an NFT up for bidding:

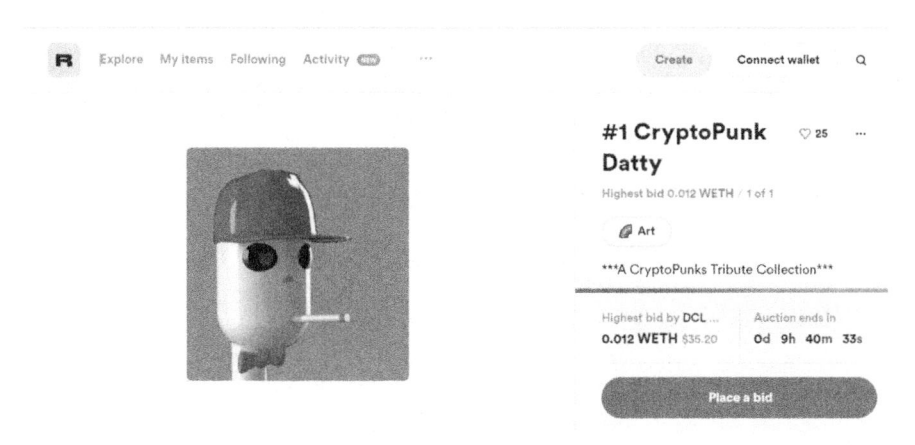

#1 CryptoPunk Datty. Rarible, by JrDat, 2021.

How NFTs Can Be Utilized for Book Launching

Authors can benefit from NFTs during a book launch. NFTs can be used not only to promote your book but to generate additional revenues both in the short term and long term. The use of NFTs will expose your book on social media when readers discuss the NFTs of your book. Of course, you'll gain fans in the process.

Here's a step-by-step guide on how to make the NFTs:

1. The first step is to choose a platform like Rarible or OpenSea where you can create the NFTs. I'm using Rarible so I can just pick "Multiple" to create one collectible multiple times. I took a screenshot so you can see it for yourself.

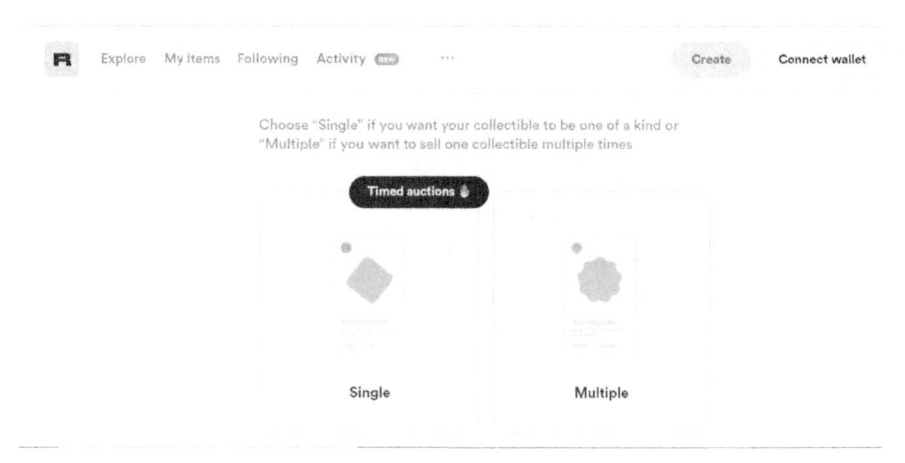

Screenshot of Rarible, Rarible (n.d.) https://rarible.com/create.

2. Then, I'll create 3 tiers (Gold, Silver, Bronze) of NFTs for the book.

3. I'll assign a limited number of NFTs for each tier like 5 Gold NFTs, 15 Silver NFTs, and 50 Bronze NFTs.

4. I'll list the NFTs for sale and offer them at different prices during my book launch. The Gold NFTs will be at $ 1,000. The Silver NFTs will be at $700 and the Bronze NFTs at $200.

5. I'll also assign a set of corresponding rewards for readers who will purchase an NFT. Let's say, a purchaser gets a bronze NFT, they'll get a copy of the ebook or a physical copy of the book. If they get a silver NFT, they'll get a copy of the ebook plus a t-shirt and a podcast. Authors can be creative in combining the rewards so they will be appealing to the readers.

Bitcoin and Blockchain for Beginners Book NFTs

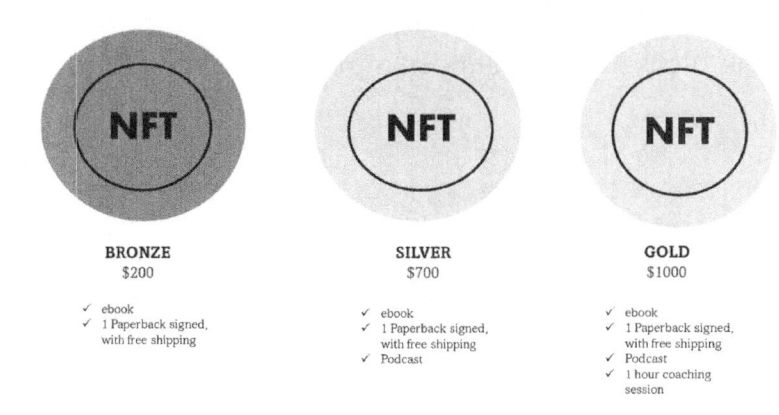

BRONZE
$200
- ebook
- 1 Paperback signed, with free shipping

SILVER
$700
- ebook
- 1 Paperback signed, with free shipping
- Podcast

GOLD
$1000
- ebook
- 1 Paperback signed, with free shipping
- Podcast
- 1 hour coaching session

6. The last step is to coordinate with the buyers for arranging the transfer of NFTs to their accounts and sending them the rewards or bonuses that go along with the NFTs.

On a final thought, NFTs are going to change the landscape for book launching in the near future. This is something book authors can look forward to.

Impact of NFTs on the Arts

Traditional representations of art like paintings, sculptures, and other physical objects may already be things of the past as NFTs are becoming the craze of Gen Z and millennials.

NFTs, just like bitcoins and blockchain, are revolutionizing the art industry. Artists can now create, sell, trade, and monetize crypto-collectibles. NFTs are proof of ownership since the artist can encode their identifying information into the smart contract. NFTs provide artists with unique and clear proof of ownership and authorship. This feature makes NFTs a great solution to avoid counterfeiting and fraud. Since NFTs are inside the blockchain, it's almost impossible to replicate them.

CHAPTER 16

ADOPTION AND THE FUTURE

Trends are important. They're proof of progress and experimentation. In whatever aspect of life, whether education, health, finance, or fashion, keeping up with the trends will help us get the best updates to guide us in our future decisions. The same thing goes for our dealings in cryptocurrencies. Innovations should not stop.

Bitcoins and blockchains need continuous improvement and upgrading to cope with industry demands. As more individuals, banking institutions, and governments get involved in bitcoins and blockchains, the need to advance is inevitable.

This chapter focuses on current trends in bitcoins, such as bitcoin halving, bitcoin in the gaming industry, upgrades in scalability and privacy, and many more. Take your time and slowly but heartily digest the information provided.

Current Trends in Cryptocurrencies

Bitcoin Halving

New bitcoins are constantly introduced into circulation through block rewards. These rewards are produced by miners who use expensive electronic equipment to solve encrypted puzzles during a block validation. After every 210,000 blocks or after every 4 years, the total number of bitcoins that miners can possibly get is halved or divided into two. This will continually happen until all 21 million bitcoins are completely mined.

The first halving of bitcoin took place in 2012. This caused the division of the reward for a mining block from 50 BTC to 25 BTC. In 2016, bitcoin halving took place causing the reward to be cut to 12.5 BTC. The last bitcoin halving took place on May 11, 2020, just 6.25 BTC were created. The next bitcoin halving will be expected in 2024. This is something miners should anticipate as it will likely result in an instantaneous drop in revenues.

Bitcoin halving often comes with some degree of turbulence in cryptocurrencies. We don't really know why Satoshi Nakomoto designed the system this way. Perhaps they were thinking that the scarcity would most likely increase the value of bitcoins to be mined. Hence, halving is good to ensure profits. But this is just my own opinion.

In an article written by Luke Conway in Investopedia, the theory of halving and the chain reaction is explained like this: When the reward is halved, this will result in a halving of the inflation as well. Then, there's lower available supply causing higher demand and consequently higher prices. Even if miners get smaller rewards, this is immaterial since the value of bitcoin increases in the process (Conway, 2021).

What Happens When We Run Out of Bitcoins?

By the year 2140, the last of the 21 million bitcoins will have been mined. There'll be no new bitcoins. Miners can still get rewards for every block they validate. However, their reward will come from transaction fees. There's still a possibility that the blockchain will be upgraded to accommodate a larger volume of bitcoins.

Effect of Bitcoin Halving

With bitcoin halving, the price of BTC is expected to skyrocket. Traders and miners might not like this idea of bitcoin halving but Satoshi Nakomoto made this possible to keep bitcoins resistant to inflation and to maintain the value of the coins. Small miners will be most affected since halving makes the business less profitable. However, global players like big "mining cartels" may strengthen their position in the market.

Upgrades in Scalability and Anonymity

Continuous upgrades in bitcoin and blockchain technology are underway. These improvements are necessary for bitcoin to maintain its progress as the new monetary system.

Lightning Network

In 2020, Lightning Network, an innovative way to handle transactions without the need for verification, was launched. This provided a second layer of security built to make transactions faster, cheaper, and more private. Watchtowers were also implemented to monitor bitcoin's Lightning Network channel for any types of breaches. Once a breach is detected, the Watchtowers will automatically release a "penalty" that will revert the funds back to the offline mode.

PayJoin and CoinSwap

PayJoin and CoinSwap are protocols built to increase the anonymity of bitcoin transactions. Bitcoin transactions are not completely private. They're only pseudo-anonymous. This makes the tracking of users possible.

With PayJoin and CoinSwap, users can send funds to themselves while at the same time receiving funds from the actual receiver. This mechanism serves as a trick for anyone trying to track the funds.

Taproot

Taproot is a major upgrade to the bitcoin protocol as it gives bitcoin more scalability, exchangeability, and anonymity. Taproot would also make smart contracts appear like regular bitcoin transactions. Taproot also utilizes the algorithm Schnorr signature, a signature scheme inking public and private keys together.

Bitcoin Vaults

Bitcoin vaults are smart contracts that would ask for several confirmations and a time delay for every bitcoin transaction. This mechanism allows a potential victim of stolen bitcoins to reverse the transaction and re-possess the stolen bitcoins.

There are more exciting innovations and developments for bitcoin and blockchain technology that we can look forward to. These are essential to the upkeep of the entire system and to realize the full mainstreaming of cryptocurrencies.

Bitcoin as Digital Gold

History taught us that gold has always been considered a thing of high value. Why is this so? Well, everyone agreed that gold has some value although it's just a shiny piece of metal.

For one thing, gold is scarce. The limited amount of gold and the fact that it's difficult to find and extract makes it very expensive. Gold is also malleable, stable, and doesn't devalue.

All these qualities make gold a treasured commodity.

Bitcoin has, more or less, the same characteristics as that gold. Bitcoin is also limited in number. It can be broken down into smaller units, it's stable, and it's highly impossible to counterfeit it. On top of these, Bitcoin can be moved easily from one person to another at any time and to any point in the globe. Some people claim that bitcoin is like gold, but better. Bitcoin, being fully digital, makes transactions in a matter of seconds.

With bitcoin being accessible, decentralized, anonymous, and secured, there's a fat chance that bitcoin will replace gold.

Bitcoin and Gaming

The gaming industry has always been at the forefront of technological innovations. With bitcoin and blockchain becoming more popular, the gaming sector embraces the likelihood of fusing gaming platforms and that blockchain technology to improve their products. What could be some of these key applications?

Advantages of Using Bitcoin in Gaming

Many video game companies include BTC as a form of payment aside from the fiat currency. This stance is shooting two birds with one stone. They get to be paid for the gaming products they offer plus they also earn bitcoins. Gamers using blockchain platforms can also store their in-game assets in reliable bitcoin wallets. Other advantages include greater security, faster transaction time, and lesser transaction fees.

Bitcoin-Inspired Games

The bitcoin-blockchain saga inspired some game developers to create games like Bitcoin Flip, Merge Cats, Spells of Genesis, Altcoin Fantasy, and some others. Bitcoin Flip and Altcoin Fantasy are trading simulators. These games offer real-time prices and several tools to make the trading more realistic. You can practice buying and selling your crypto assets through these games. You get to enjoy and at the same time, you learn all the basics of bitcoin trading. As for Merge Cats and Spells of Genesis, bitcoins and other cryptocurrencies are offered as rewards.

Blockchain's Impact on Industries

The amazing mechanism of blockchain brings a fresh look at technology. People are slowly beginning to see its importance due to its ability to modernize industries. It finally dawned on people that this advanced technology can be leveraged by the different sectors not only in finance and trading. Blockchain technology is slowly being mainstreamed in almost all sectors including banking, manufacturing, health, and even governments.

Industries Leveraging the Blockchain

According to the PwC's Global Blockchain Survey (Sanka, et.al.), Blockchain technology is mostly adopted by the financial service sector. This is apparently due to the steady growth of cryptocurrencies with more blockchain wallet users turning toward this new monetary system. This technology has significantly altered the landscape of the business sectors. Tokens are now being used to represent virtual assets. Initial Coin Offerings (ICOs) are also being utilized as an alternative to debt or capital funding offered by banks and private lending institutions.

The Banking Sector

The banking sector is moving towards adopting blockchain technology for cross-border payments and trading. Blockchain technology will fast-track transactions, cutting through third parties and other unnecessary procedures. It will likewise provide transparency and mitigation of data redundancy.

The Manufacturing Industry

Blockchain technology is promising even in the manufacturing industries. Simplification of the manufacturing process is made possible by integrating blockchain technology in supply chain management to monitor containers out for shipping. Companies involved in manufacturing food products utilize blockchain technology for quality and integrity checks.

The Health Sector

Even the medical and health sector sees an opportunity in blockchain technology to be used in supply and medicine verification, and identification of counterfeit drugs. Blockchain technology can likewise be used in facilitating data collaborations toward a better and more accurate diagnosis of illness. It also reduces manual administrative tasks leading to increased work efficiency and cost reduction.

The Aviation Industry

The aviation industry is looking into the possible benefits of blockchain technology in automating processes and loyalty program transactions, ticketing, and bookkeeping.

The Construction Industry

Blockchain technology is being explored to streamline project management. Smart contracts would also improve efficiency and resolve conflicts even before they surface and can hold parties more accountable and involved in the project. Experts are also looking into the possibility of combining blockchain and building information modeling (BIM) technologies to enhance the effectiveness of smart contracts.

The Government and the Public Sector

Different governments across the globe are discovering the benefits of blockchain technology. This can prevent fraudulent transactions, reduce paperwork and operational costs, and increase work efficiency and accountability.

A blockchain-powered government can result in advantages like:

- Securing data storage of government, citizen, and public dealings.

- Reducing manual and administrative work.

- Reducing corruption and abuse.

- Reducing work redundancy and excessive expenditures.

Blockchain's DLT can be utilized to facilitate a wide spectrum of government and public functions like digital payment, land registration, tax payment, identity management, voting, health care, and a lot more.

The Role of Women in Bitcoin and Blockchain Technology

What once has been a male-dominated venture is now welcoming to women. Bitcoin knows no bounds. It doesn't discriminate against any race. It knows no age nor gender.

Over time, there's a rising number of women crypto users and investors. Several cryptocurrency exchanges have reported an increase in the number of women traders. This number may even rise in the future.

Women like Hester Peirce, Rhia Bhutoria, Camila Russo, and Caitlin Long are achieving success in cryptocurrencies. They have earned every right to be in their current positions now. They have been making big waves in the crypto-sphere with their advocacies and innovations for cryptocurrencies. They're the leaders and shapers that we need in the industry. Women are more likely to become long-term investors. They're less impulsive and they tend to hold on to their positions. This explains why more women are over-indexed on bitcoins (Grayscale Investments, 2019).

Historically, women are less confident when it comes to managing their finances (Allianz Life, 2019). However, crypto investments offer women more freedom to explore areas to improve their financial status. It's a great way for them to start accumulating crypto assets and have access to a new marketplace. The features of cryptocurrencies like decentralization, anonymity, and security enable women to be more confident and independent in their financial ventures. Yes, cryptocurrencies are bringing out women's innate financial abilities. No longer are women constrained to be home managers but they're turning into successful developers, miners, traders, and investors of cryptocurrencies.

On a final note, for the crypto industry to flourish, it must take both men's and women's perspectives into account. Both men and women are indispensable in policymaking, technology development, crypto trading, and decision-making. The industry must promote practices that foster the acceptance of women entrepreneurs in the world of cryptocurrency and blockchain.

How Cryptocurrency and Blockchain Are Changing the Financial Industry

Because of how blockchain was written, it is able to focus on the development and even the startup of solutions that are not going to be able to be done by those who are working in the financial industry. Not just that, but blockchain supports cryptocurrency and any services that are needed to support the use of cryptocurrency. Blockchain also enables financial assets to be tracked inside of an environment that is completely secure and you do not have to worry about it being hacked or changed. Not to mention, the complexity of the transaction process is going to be reduced.

Blockchain makes it better and easier to manage the digital risks that are always going to be there for the financial industry. Ledgers are going to be created and sent out to those who need to see the ledgers and they are not going to be sent to anyone else. The processes that are being used when dealing with the risks are going to be sent to these people as well. On top of it all, it improves the processes that are in place for the networks that are needed in order to verify the history of any transaction that has been done.

Bitcoin was on the rise in 2012, and about 1 billion dollars were sent through the system. Ever since then, more have been sent through the system and it is used more. There are a few companies that are trying to break into the Bitcoin market, while others are trying to improve the services that they currently offer to their customers so that they can try and keep their customers and make their banking experience better. Sadly, all banks, no matter who they are, are afraid to break into the full use of blockchain because they are afraid of what it is going to do to their services and how it is going to affect their customers.

However, technology is constantly evolving and it is reducing the fees that are in place for a lot of financial transactions that are done daily. Not only that but also the risks that are involved with these transactions are being reduced when it comes to the exchanging of currency. Any payment faults or cut-off times are going to be eliminated because there is no longer going to be the need to have duplicate documentation. So, there is yet another added benefit: that you are going to be reducing the amount of paperwork that is printed out!

Those financial institutions that do invest with blockchain are having to set up teams that are inside of their branches so that they can deal with any startup companies that are going to want to use blockchain.

There are a lot of common mistakes that Bitcoin is going to get rid of within the financial industry. Thanks to the fact that blockchain can handle payments, there is a living document that the user can view in order to see when their payment is due and what is being paid out of the payment that they make. The need to have documentation is going to be eliminated as well because the documents are going to be saved on a node that is going to be accessed by the bank and by the customer.

When dealing with startup companies, blockchain is going to use a series of projections that are going to show a financial service if they are going to want to invest in that company or not. This is going to make it easier for the bank to evaluate their risks and know if they are going to want to loan out money or not. Therefore, banks are going to be out less money than if they did not use blockchain and the traditional ways that they evaluate risk.

Cryptos in the Next Decade

We have a clear and bright portrait of the future of cryptocurrencies. Currently, cryptocurrencies are utilized as both assets and mediums for daily transactions. More institutional investors are excited to join the bandwagon and make profits from the volatility of cryptocurrencies.

The innovations and developments in Bitcoin's blockchain and Ethereum's blockchain prove that cryptocurrencies can last not only a decade but a couple or more. As regulations by governments around the world keep up with the pace, the crypto ecosystem will likely expand and flourish. This can mean an explosion of low-cost and fast transactions that will revolutionize value exchange just like the Internet has revolutionized information.

The institutional adoption of Bitcoin and blockchain has already begun from gaming to payments, banking, health, manufacturing, and business sectors. By the end of the decade, most financial technology (FinTech) companies will already have a crypto component. Governments and the public sector will also transition into the cryptosphere by integrating blockchain technology in different government services like health care, land registration, insurance, policymaking, administrative work, identification processing system, etc.

The next decade looks promising for Bitcoin, as well. It's forecasted that there'll be more mainstream acceptance as big global entities and the central banks compete with one another in their accumulation of bitcoins and other cryptocurrencies. More importantly, there'll be stringent regulations of crypto trading by various influential countries.

CONCLUSION

Cryptocurrency has a lot that you need to know, a lot you need to take into consideration, and a lot of factors that you will have to decide for yourself. A few years ago, there weren't many choices you could make, but with an ever-growing, advancing world, there are more choices than you can even comprehend. Information is your greatest ally; and the best part? Most of it is freely available for you. All you need to learn is to filter truth from false and work your way from there.

Although it is good to listen to the advice of others, it is best to adapt your choices to suit your circumstances (a factor many people tend to forget when pushing you to make a decision). When it comes to cryptocurrency, you have to take responsibility for your decisions, because despite having followed someone else's bad advice, it is ultimately you that are going to lose the money. So, isn't it best to have no one but yourself to blame if losses are incurred by a mistake you made? It is far worse to have fallen for a scam, or blindly followed a tip that ultimately caused your failure, especially if you would have chosen differently, had you decided to be in control.

Furthermore, cryptocurrencies are volatile by nature. Everywhere you go and look, this factor pops up. So much so, that it would be foolish to ignore it (although too many people still do). And so, it is best to invest only money you can actually afford to lose. In fact, it is best that cryptocurrency does not make up the entirety of your investments, but just a small part. Apart from its potentially high returns, you have a greater chance for higher losses. If those losses do occur, you may not feel it as much if you have invested in other options as well. Again, how you diversify your portfolio is all up to you. It is officially in your hands, and who knows where this pathway will take you.

When starting off, remember to take it slowly. Diving into the deep end of the pool will do no one any favors as the risk of loss can certainly outweigh the learning process that comes with it. Don't consider letting yourself into the deep end this time, with cryptocurrency, you are far more likely to drown than with a different investment.

Finally, learn to have fun with it. Taking on cryptocurrency out of a need or pure desire to earn will bring nothing but stress and problems. Rather, find ways to enjoy it, set up achievable goals, and make bets with yourself. Challenge yourself to learn as much as you can about crypto, and take losses with the mindset of learning. Don't give in to defeat or panic.

Remember that research and patience are your two greatest

allies when it comes to the world of cryptocurrency. Avoid hurdles, such as peer pressure, common scams, and poor investment choices. Having both the dedication and patience to do research is one of the primary characteristics of a savvy trader.

Now you have the foundational knowledge of crypto, as well as the key steps to start your trading journey, don't hesitate to start today, whether by paper simulations or small trades that you can afford to lose if the worst occurs. Remember, the harder you work, the better your chances of success. Practice makes perfect after all. And the scariest reality is the factor that just putting a little extra effort already gets you the edge over most other investors, who tend to walk into these things blindly.

However, please do keep in mind that this book is designed for educational purposes, and not meant to be professional/financial recommendations. That means that although the information is intended to help your trading journey, it is not guaranteed to help you succeed.

Still, everything given here is meant to help you grow. Cryptocurrency is no easy feat, but many people want to take part in it because it is growing in prominence and importance. There are still many factors holding people back, such as its volatile nature. But if you are willing to take on the risk, then you will be participating in the rise of a new digital era.

A Few Acronyms and Sayings

- **AES:** Hardware encryption.

- **AMM:** Automated Market Makers are autonomous trading machines, their mechanisms enable decentralized exchanges (DEX), see Chapter 15.

- **API id:** Application Programming Interface, is a unique code that identifies and authenticates a program, a user, or a developer.

- **AVM:** Ethereum Virtual Machine.

- **Bagholder:** Somebody that bought near the peak and held investment during a decline, in this way losing a lot of money.

- **Bear market:** When the financial market is losing value.

- **Bear whale market:** When someone sells large amounts of cryptocurrency to create a large loss in the market.

- **BSc:** Binance Smart Chain.

- **BscScan:** It is a blockchain explorer that allows interaction through its platform with Binance Smart Chain, here one can find information on DeFi projects built on BSC.

- **DdoS:** Distributed Denial of Service, is a type of attack aimed at collapsing a Network, or a website by sending them so many requests that the infrastructure crashes.

- **DeFi:** Decentralized finance, see Chapter 15.

- **DLT:** Distributed Ledger Technologies is a decentralized ledger, we will hear about this kind of solution in the future.

- **ETC:** Ethereum classic.

- **Etherscan:** System to check in a transaction in a blockchain node.

- **Ethplorer:** Ethplorer provides the tools needed to track smart transactions and contracts on the Ethereum blockchain.

- **FOMO:** Fear Of Missing Out, when people fear that they will not be able to participate in something important, e.g., a big gain.

- **FUD:** Fear, Uncertainty, Doubt, when people are afraid of losing a lot, e.g., a heavy loss.

- **GIT:** Is an open-source, free software used to track changes in the files, it is used for software development, it is very fast, easy to use, supports distributed and non-linear jobs, and gives integrity to data.

- **Hashrate:** It is the power of the hardware used for mining, measured in the number of calculations per second (hashes per second TH/s or GH/s).

- **Hodl:** Among crypto-trading enthusiasts means Hold On for Dear Life.

- **ICO:** Initial Coin Offering. It is a way to collect funds for an organization that wants to create a service or currency.

- **Joke coin:** Joke coin has similar purposes to a meme coin.

- **KYC:** Know Your Customer. These are procedures that allow the identification of those who register, in banking and finance. In many parts of the world, it is required by law. The purpose is to have certain data and the identity of those who want to register, in other areas it is done for commercial purposes.

- **Limit order:** A limit order is an order to buy or sell a share, fiat, cryptocurrency, or other financial product, at a specific or more advantageous price for the issuer, the market will decide whether or not to accept the request

- **Long position:** Long position is a bullish attitude. In practice when one buys a product, an asset expects an increase in value in the medium to long term.

- **Market cap:** Known in the stock market as market capitalization, in the cryptocurrency market it is the market value of outstanding cryptocurrencies. To find out how much the market capitalization is, you need to multiply the crypto price by the number of cryptocurrencies in circulation.

- **Meme coin:** Meme coins are used to publicize and spread a particular blockchain or network.

- **Mempool:** Is a temporary buffer in which unconfirmed or suspended user transactions are stored; it is from here that the miner selects, processes, and integrates into the blockchain. A transaction is removed from the mempool when it is confirmed and placed in a block.

- **MEW:** MyEther Wallet is a cryptocurrency wallet, see Chapter 12.

- **Moon:** When a cryptocurrency tends to be particularly bullish, one can find this expression or its verb, mooning, to signal the possibility of its evolution.

- **MyCripto:** A useful tool for safely managing one's Ethereum accounts.

- **PEG:** This is a term used in reference to the relationship between a token and a stablecoin. It is the specific price a token wishes to hold against a given stablecoin or fiat money.

- **Pump and dump:** Is a scheme designed to increase the price of a share, cryptocurrency, or other, whose strategy consists of spreading false recommendations based on exaggerated or aberrant statements through various communication channels.

- **Shilling:** This is when someone vigorously and maliciously advertises a cryptocurrency to inflate its value and attract new investors to it. These people, known as shills, aim to increase the value of the cryptocurrency to profit from it, see also "pump and dump."

- **Short position:** Is created when a trader first sells a security to buy it back or hedge it later at a lower price. It is a practice used in forex trading and in equity products and cryptocurrencies.

- **Slippage tolerance:** This is the percentage that you are ready to accept during a Swap on AMM, this cost is the difference between the actual price of the transaction and the price quoted at the order confirmation.

- **Soft fork:** This is an update that integrates with existing software and communicates with software not updated, programs evolutions and new rules that do not conflict with previous ones, and allows nodes not updated to be able to update, all this without creating problems to the network.

- **Source code:** The original programming language.

- **SPV:** Simplified Payment Verification, permits checking whether a transaction is present on the Bitcoin blockchain by downloading block headers.

- **Stablecoin:** Stable currencies tend to align with fiat currencies, even if they have minimal fluctuations in value, during high volatility markets they keep the exchange rate with the fiat currencies they are pegged to swap.

- **Tag/Memo:** A large number of centralized exchanges use Destination Tag technology. If cryptocurrency traders use it, a Tag/Memo is used to identify the individual account and reference it for a given transaction.

- **Tron:** Tron is a decentralized blockchain-based digital platform, Tronix (TRX) is Tron's cryptocurrency.

- **Whale:** Cryptocurrency whales are those who hold huge amounts of cryptocurrency, amounts sufficient to significantly move the value of cryptocurrency.

Thank you for choosing this book.

Would you recommend this book to a friend?

I invite you to leave a review.

If you prefer to contact us in private to give us suggestions, you can write to : **new.book.action@gmail.com**.

To be informed about new publications, please write to **new.book.action@gmail.com**.

OTHER WORKS BY THE SAME AUTHOR

Forex Trade Market Get Money

© Copyright 2022 All Rights Reserved.

Reference Number: 18490130922S064